Secret of the
SHARK PIT

Secret of the SHARK PIT

Lee Roddy

PUBLISHING
Pomona, California

SECRET OF THE SHARK PIT
Copyright © 1988 by Lee Roddy

Library of Congress Cataloging-in-Publication Data

Roddy, Lee, 1921—
Secret of the shark pit.

Summary: Several acts of disobedience against his
father's orders plunge twelve-year-old Josh into terrible
trouble during a search for a long-lost Hawaiian treasure
guarded by sharks.
  [1. Buried treasure—Fiction. 2. Hawaii—Fiction.
3. Obedience—Fiction. 4. Mystery and detective stories.]
I. Title.
PZ7.R6Se 1988   [Fic]   88-45300
ISBN 0-929608-14-3

Published by Focus on the Family Publishing, Pomona, California 91799.
Distributed by Word Books, Waco, Texas.

Scripture quotations are taken from the Holy Bible, New International Version
copyright © 1973, 1978, 1984 International Bible Society.

Editor: S. Rickly Christian
Designer: Sherry Nicolai Russell
Cover Illustration: Ernest Norcia

Printed in the United States of America

89 90 91 92 93 / 10 9 8 7 6 5 4 3

*To Cicely, my wife of forty years,
whose unfailing faith, encouragement and love
helped achieve my boyhood dream of
becoming an author of books that make a difference.*

CONTENTS

Chapter One

QUESTIONS FROM A STRANGER

Even after six months, Joshua Ladd was so lonely he still hurt inside. The pain of missing his best friend would not go away, no matter what parents and teachers said. That, along with his worsening allergy to the smog, made his life miserable.

One late spring afternoon, the normally fast-moving sixth grader shuffled alone from school toward his San Fernando Valley home. The smog-shrouded mountains ringing Los Angeles to the north rose blue-gray before him, making it hard to breathe.

"I'd give anything to see Tank!" he told himself fiercely as he took a shortcut across a vacant lot filled with junk and high brown weeds. "There's got to be a way! Maybe even a way we could go to school together again."

Josh glimpsed his brother and sister through an opening in the high concrete block wall that marked the end of the vacant lot. Tiffany had just stepped off the high school bus as her younger brother, Nathan, walked by on his way home from elementary school. Josh could see them laughing and talking. Their happiness made Josh more lonely.

Josh and Tank Catlett had been friends since they were babies. Because their parents had been close, the two boys had often been together in the same playpen. From the time they entered school, Josh and Tank were like brothers. Then Mr. Catlett was promoted as manager of a chain department store and moved to Hawaii, taking Tank and all his family.

"It's not fair!" Josh told himself with a heavy sigh. He angrily kicked an old soft drink can. It sailed ahead of him and clattered against the pinkish-colored block wall beside the residential street. As Josh neared the sidewalk, a man suddenly stepped out from an opening in the wall.

"Hey, kid!"

Josh glanced around and slowed. He was big for his twelve years, with broad shoulders from years of swimming. He was not much afraid of anything, especially in broad daylight with his brother and sister within yelling distance. Still, Josh's parents had taught him to be wary of strangers.

He stopped at the edge of the vacant lot, well out of arm's reach of the stranger. "Yeah?" Josh asked. He automatically brushed wavy brown hair back from his intensely blue eyes.

The stranger was a big, powerfully built man in his late thirties. He wore wraparound sunglasses and a dark three-piece suit. "Kid, I'm looking for somebody," the stranger said, reaching into his breast pocket and producing a photo. Another slid out and fluttered onto the edge of the vacant lot.

In his customarily quick fashion, Josh bent to pick up the picture.

"It's okay, kid! I'll get it!" the stranger exclaimed, reaching down so fast that he knocked Josh slightly off balance.

"I've already got it," Josh said, coughing as he stood back up. Even that little bit of sudden activity made his allergy act up and his chest hurt. Josh glanced at the color photograph. He caught a glimpse of some strange-looking cliffs rising out of a small blue-green bay. Two dome-like rounded objects stood on top of the cliffs, but he could not tell what they were. They vaguely reminded Josh of some unusual rock formations.

"Gimme that!" the man snapped angrily as he snatched the picture away.

"I'm sorry, mister! I was just trying to—"

"It's okay! Forget it!" The man's manner changed and he managed a half-smile. He slid the color picture into the inside jacket pocket with his right hand. With his left, he shoved the first picture back toward Josh. "You know this man?" he asked.

Josh's eyes dipped to the photo. His heart gave a lurch.

"Well?" the well-dressed man demanded impatiently.

Josh glanced sharply at the man's eyes. The boy could only see his own reflection in the dark wraparound sunglasses. "Why do you want to know?" he asked evasively.

The man's mouth popped open so fast Josh thought he was going to get yelled at. Instead, the man said with controlled quietness, "He's an old army buddy. I've heard he lives around here."

Josh's eyes narrowed suspiciously and he backed up a half-step. "Army buddy?"

"Yeah! I want to surprise him after all these years. You know him?"

The boy's mind raced. He turned to see his brother and sister getting farther and farther away. "Sorry, mister! I've got to catch up with my friends."

Josh turned and ran hard down the sidewalk after his siblings.* He heard the man swearing behind him.

Josh panted up to Tiffany and Nathan just as they waved goodbye to the last of their friends and headed toward their home around the corner at the far end of the block.

"Guess what?" Josh asked, sliding between fourteen-year-old Tiffany and ten-year-old Nathan. Josh's chest burned from inhaling the smog during his run, but he ignored the discomfort and tried not to wheeze. He turned to glance back. The mysterious stranger was gone.

"You got kept after school for disobeying the teacher again," Tiffany said with a shrug. She was quite tall and

---

*The definition and pronunciation of words marked by an asterisk are contained in a glossary at the end of the book.

very slender, with short brunette hair. "You're going to get in big trouble someday for that," she warned.

"Yeah," Nathan agreed. "Like you're not supposed to cut across that vacant lot. I saw you! You know what Dad would do to you if he knew?"

Nathan could be very annoying at times, but Josh was too excited to reply just now. "Forget that! The reason I was running—"

"It doesn't matter why!" Tiffany interrupted. "You're not supposed to exert yourself! You'll end up in the emergency room again!"

"Never mind that!" Josh cried.

Nathan was suddenly suspicious. "Just why were you running so hard?" The little brother was the smallest kid in his class.

Josh ignored the questions. "Let's cut across between these two houses," he said.

"What for?" Tiffany demanded, with a big sister's automatic habit of taking command. "Who's after you?"

Josh peered back through the afternoon smog. "Not after me. After Dad!"

"Who's after Dad?" Tiffany asked, turning to look back the way Josh was staring.

"And why?" Nathan asked. He shifted his backpack of books on his shoulder and shaded his eyes against the sun.

"I don't know!" Josh admitted. He steered his reluctant siblings off the sidewalk and between the only houses that didn't have fences. Quickly, he told them about the stranger.

When he finished, Tiffany shook her head. "That doesn't make any sense! Dad never was in the army!"

"Exactly!" Josh exclaimed as they emerged from between the two houses and crossed the alley. "But he had Dad's picture!" Frowning, Nathan pushed open the back gate through the high block wall fence into the Ladds' backyard. "Why would anyone have Dad's picture—and lie about it?" he asked.

"That's what I'd like to know!" Josh replied. "There's something strange going on!"

Tiffany stopped on the back steps of the Ladds' used-brick ranch-style tract home. "Oh, Josh! You're always thinking something strange is going on!"

Before Josh could protest, their mother called from the kitchen, "Children! Quiet, please! I'm on the phone with Barbara Catlett!"

"From Hawaii?" Tiffany whooped. "Can I talk to Marsha?" She was Tank's older sister.

"And I want to talk to Tank!" Josh yelled. The two older Ladd kids dashed into the house and down the long hallway toward the living room phone.

"Children, please!" Mrs. Ladd called from the kitchen.

Tiffany beat Josh to the phone. She snatched it up from the small table by their father's big chair and cried excitedly, "Mrs. Catlett? Is Marsha home?" Josh watched Tiffany's face sink as she reluctantly handed the phone to him. "Marsha isn't around, and Mom's gone to get an address for Mrs. Catlett. So they say you and Tank can talk a moment."

Josh grabbed the phone and almost yelled into it. "Tank?"

"Josh! Hi!" The familiar voice came across the wire. Tank was a slow-talking, deliberate person whose total contrast to Josh made them unlikely friends.

As Tiffany headed for the kitchen, Josh slid into the big chair and eased his feet onto the footrest. It automatically popped out as he leaned back. "Tank, you sound as though you're right down the street!"

"Well,..." Tank replied, dragging out the word and then adding with his usual maddening slowness, "Hawaii's only about twenty-five hundred miles by air, you know."

Maddeningly slow or not, it was a voice that Josh greatly missed. "I sure wish you were back here, Tank! It's so lonesome!"

Tank said sadly, "It's worse here!"

"But your parents told my folks that you're making lots of new friends in Honolulu!"

"They are, but I'm not! I'm the only haole* in my whole class."

"How-lee? What's that?"

"Hawaiian word. It used to mean stranger, but now people here use it to mean a white person."

"I remember my folks talking about the—what'd they

call it?—Oh! The 'rainbow of colors' of people living in Hawaii. White-, brown-, black-, yellow- and red-skinned . . ."

Tank interrupted. "For the first time in my life, I know what it's like to be a minority." Tank's slow voice sounded miserable as he continued. "Most of the kids are real nice, so it's not really my skin that's the problem. It's just that they've known each other for years, but I'm the new kid and the only one whose skin is really different. Josh, I'd give anything if you could be here with me."

Josh could only say softly, "Me, too, Tank."

His friend changed the subject. "How's your allergy?"

"Gets worse and worse every summer. But I'll survive, I hope. I wish we could move back to the beach like when we were kids. No smog there."

"You could move to Hawaii and breathe this air."

"Don't I wish!"

"Hey!" Tank's tone brightened. "Guess what?"

"What?"

Tank lowered his voice. "If you can come here, I've got a secret place to explore! Even the kamaainas* don't know about it."

"The *what?*"

"Kamaainas, or natives." Tank replied.

Josh's spirits lifted. "What's so secret about it?"

Tank whispered, "Can't tell you on the phone."

When the boys had lived next door to each other, their favorite pastime was exploring. Nothing really dangerous had ever happened, but they'd had a lot of fun pretending.

"Why not?" Josh asked, automatically whispering back.

"Because it could be dangerous!"

"Then write me a letter."

"Can't do that, either! Boy! If you could get over here on summer vacation. . ."

Mrs. Ladd broke in from the kitchen phone. "I'm back. Tank, please put your mother on the line and you boys say goodbye."

Josh reluctantly obeyed. From the kitchen, he could hear Tiffany pleading to talk to Marsha, Tank's older sister.

Josh was frustrated and excited. His mind raced. What kind of secret could Tank have? Josh leaned back hard into his father's favorite chair. "There's got to be a way to visit Tank!" he exclaimed aloud.

He heard his father's key in the front door lock. Josh jumped up just as his father entered from the hallway carrying his briefcase. John Ladd was a nice-looking, six-foot-tall man with dark wavy hair. He was a high school history teacher.

Tank Catlett's father had once laughingly described John Ladd and his son Josh as being "like two warm bottles of soda water that somebody shook up real hard and then yanked off the caps; only these two never run out of spizzy."

"Hey, Dad, guess what?" Josh said excitedly,

"Mrs. Catlett is on the phone! And you know what else? On the way home from school today, some guy—"

"The Catletts are on the phone? I was going to call Sam tonight." Mr. Ladd handed his scarred brown leather briefcase to Josh. "Here, please put this in my study while I grab the phone."

"Okay. But Dad, about this guy. . ."

"In a minute, Son." Mr. Ladd dropped into the big upholstered chair. He scooped up the phone. "Barbara? It's John! How's Sam? Great! Is he home? Well, when he comes in, please tell him he doesn't know how fortunate all of you are to be out of here! Every year it gets worse!"

Josh started down the hallway. He met his sister coming from the kitchen. Josh muttered, "Why do the grown-ups always get to talk and we kids don't?"

"Because," Tiffany said with an older sister's slightly superior air as she opened her bedroom door, "they pay the phone bills."

Josh didn't feel like answering. He could hear his father's voice down the hallway.

"I had to drive to downtown Los Angeles today. It was terrible! Smog, heat and bumper-to-bumper freeway traffic both ways. But I've got news that I haven't had time to tell my wife yet."

Josh tuned out his father's voice as his mind jumped back to Tank. "It's not fair! We're both lonely." He opened the hall door to the combination den and study.

"I wonder if Tank's right? Maybe I could breathe better in Hawaii."

As Josh set the briefcase on the tidy desk, he heard Nathan shriek. Josh turned and raced into the hallway, almost colliding with Tiffany rushing from her room.

Nathan bolted from the kitchen door toward them, wildly waving a peanut butter and jelly sandwich. His eyes were wide and he was making sputtering noises.

"What's the matter?" Tiffany demanded, taking charge as usual. "Are you choking?"

Nathan shook his head violently, swallowed hard and yelled, "We're going to Hawaii!"

Chapter Two

THE MYSTERY DEEPENS

"**W**hat're you talking about?" Josh demanded of his little brother.

"Yes!" Tiffany added emphatically, standing under the family picture gallery in the hallway. "Talk sense!"

"It's true!" Nathan insisted, waving the sandwich toward the kitchen. "We're going to Hawaii! Ask Mom!"

The two older Ladd children rushed into the kitchen, but their mother was still on the phone and waved them to silence. She was a tall, slender woman with very black hair and a dimple in her left cheek.

"Well, Barbara," Mrs. Ladd said into the phone, "You know as much about it as I do. We'd better hang up while I get the whole story from John. We'll call you back tonight so he can talk to Sam."

After she hung up, all three Ladd kids peppered her with questions, but she shook her head and headed for the door into the dining room. "It's just as much a surprise to me as it is to you," she said. "Let's ask your father."

Mr. Ladd burst through the living room door into the

dining room. He grinned broadly and swept his wife into his arms.

"Sorry to spring the news on you like that, Mary, but as long as Barbara was on the phone, I figured I'd better tell her."

"Tell her what?" Josh cried.

"Yes!" Tiffany echoed. "What's going on?"

Mr. Ladd kept his wife in the crook of his left arm and scooped the three children close with his free arm. "Two great pieces of news! First, you remember that article I wrote for the *National Historical Journal* a couple of months ago?"

There was an answering chorus. "Yes!" John Ladd had supplemented his teacher's income with free-lance* writing as long as Josh could remember.

"Well, the editor liked it so much he asked me to come downtown and talk to him personally. Then he gave me a major assignment!"

Josh wanted his father to get to the part about Hawaii. "And?" he prompted.

Mr. Ladd paused dramatically as he sometimes did, quickly looking from one member of his family to another. Then he grinned and explained. "The editor is not only going to pay well for the article, but is also paying my expenses to Hawaii!"

"Can we go, too?" Josh asked breathlessly, thinking of being with Tank again.

"Well, the cost of my plane ticket will be covered by

the *Journal.* I've got enough total mileage from my frequent flyer* program for two free round-trip tickets. That covers three of us, and I think we can afford to take the other two of you along!"

The three children erupted in joyous shouts. Josh could hardly believe it! To see Tank again! To find out what he whispered about on the phone!

When they had calmed down a little, Tiffany asked, "Dad, what's the second piece of news?"

Mr. Ladd's happy look vanished. He leaned forward slightly. "You must all promise me one thing."

"What's that?" everyone asked together.

"Will you promise?" their father asked, glancing at each one.

The three kids nodded solemnly.

Mr. Ladd said seriously, "You may tell your friends we're going to Hawaii for vacation, but you can't mention that I'm on an article assignment."

"Why not?" Tiffany demanded, absently opening a cupboard and taking out a box of cookies. Sometimes she was awfully bossy and not very careful how she asked things, even of grown-ups.

Her mother reached over and took the package. "If your father asked you to do something, that should be enough. And no snack this close to dinner!"

"But Nathan had a sandwich!"

"Only because I was on the phone and didn't see him get it, Tiffany!"

Josh moaned, "Ah, come on! I want to hear more about going to Hawaii!"

Nathan turned toward the hallway door. "Not me! I'm going to pack right now!"

Mr. Ladd chuckled. "You don't need to do that just yet! We can't go until school's out in two weeks! Remember, you can tell your friends we're going to Hawaii, but don't say anything about my assignment!"

Mrs. Ladd suggested, "Why don't all of you go to your rooms and make lists of what you want to pack? While you're at it, please straighten your rooms, too." She added with a smile, "I'm getting afraid to go into some of them without first getting a tetanus* shot."

Josh almost floated to his room. "I'm going to Hawaii! I'm going to see Tank!"

Josh was so excited his breathing became painful. He glanced out of the window at the smoggy sky and thought, "It won't be long until I don't have to breathe this stuff! I'll be in Hawaii with Tank again! Then I can find out what's so secret he couldn't tell me or write me."

At dinner, all the talk was about plans for the trip. There was so much excitement that it wasn't until Josh was preparing for bed that he thought, "Why would Dad not want us to say anything about his assignment?"

Josh suddenly remembered the stranger. In his pajamas and robe, Josh padded down to the little den where his father was correcting papers. Mr. Ladd peered at his son over the top of his new silver-rimmed half-glasses. The glasses looked strange to the boy.

"Dad, you got a minute?"

"I always have time for my children," Mr. Ladd said. He lay down his pencil, removed the half-glasses and leaned back in his chair. "What's on your mind, Son?"

"Well," Josh said slowly, easing onto the edge of the straight-backed chair beside the small desk. "There was this stranger," he began, and then proceeded to tell the whole story. "Dad, could that man have anything to do with the assignment the magazine gave you?" he concluded.

Mr. Ladd was thoughtfully silent for a long time before answering. "Maybe. But I really don't know, Son."

"Who could he be, Dad?"

"I don't know that, either. Now tell me about the picture the stranger dropped."

"I only got a glimpse," Josh explained, and then he briefly described the color photograph. "I think what I saw were cliffs," he said.

Suddenly, Mr. Ladd stepped forward and gripped his son's forearms. "Cliffs, you said? What kind?"

"I don't know, just cliffs. Not very big, but full of... holes, maybe."

"Holes? Could they have been lava tubes*?"

"I don't know what those are."

"Did you notice anything about the tops of the cliffs?"

"There were these dome-type things," Josh said. "I've seen something like them on those nature shows we get on the educational channel. Sort of like termite hills in Africa."

Mr. Ladd released Josh's arms and spun to face his briefcase. He worked the double combination locks and raised the lid. Josh got a pleasant whiff of leather.

Mr. Ladd reached in and picked up a picture. He held it out toward Josh. "Did the stranger's photo look anything like this?"

The boy stared, and then excitedly grabbed the picture for a closer look. "That's it! It's the same place, Dad!"

Mr. Ladd said softly, "The Shark Pit!"

"The what?"

"So someone else does know!"

"Dad, what'd you say about a shark—"

"Shh!" Mr. Ladd interrupted. "Not another word!" He retrieved the picture and replaced it in his briefcase. "Now, please go back to bed and forget about this!"

Josh felt frustrated as he moved reluctantly toward his bedroom. He muttered to himself, "How can I possibly forget about it? What's going on anyway?"

No answers came. Instead, he felt a kind of rising excitement and a sense of danger he couldn't explain.

That danger was heightened when the Ladd family returned from Sunday night church services that weekend. When Josh entered their home, he found the sliding glass door to the patio had been broken. He ran yelling to his parents in the living room.

"Dad! Mom! Somebody's broken in! We've been

robbed!"

The family dashed to see the broken patio door. "Quickly!" Mr. Ladd said, "Check every room!"

It took only a few minutes to find that the entire house had been thoroughly ransacked. Mr. Ladd said, "I'll call the police! While we wait for them to arrive, go back through your rooms and see what's missing!"

Josh realized what a terrible feeling it was to know somebody had been inside your room, opening drawers, throwing things on the floor and breaking airplane and ship models he and his father had made together.

Tiffany and Nathan's rooms were also ransacked, but their parents' master bedroom and Mr. Ladd's little study had suffered the most. They were disasters. Every closet and drawer had been opened and the contents dumped on the carpet. Papers and books were scattered everywhere.

By the time two uniformed police officers arrived, the five Ladd family members had all agreed: as far as they could determine, nothing was missing.

The officers took statements and asked questions about possible suspects or motives. Mr. Ladd shook his head and shrugged, but Josh thought of something.

"Dad, what about the stranger?"

Mr. Ladd frowned, then nodded. "It doesn't seem likely, but...well, perhaps you should tell them, Josh."

The boy complied, feeling scared. When he had finished, one officer suggested that Josh go down to the police station and look at mug books* to see if he could recognize the stranger. Josh said he didn't think it would do any good because the stranger had worn dark wrap-around sunglasses.

When the police officers had gone, Josh walked out in the backyard with his father. The night was unusually chilly for Los Angeles, and Josh felt goose bumps rise on his arms and neck.

"Dad, since nothing seems to be missing, do you think the burglar will return?"

"The officers didn't think so."

"You didn't tell them anything about the Shark Pit. Do you suppose?. . ."

"The stranger already has a photo, so that's not what he was after."

"Could he have been after something else?"

Mr. Ladd blinked and looked down at his son. "You know, I hadn't thought of that!"

"Thought of what?"

"If it was the stranger that burglarized us, what else could he have been looking for?"

"So you have something else he might have wanted?"

Slowly, Mr. Ladd nodded. "But if that's it, he won't find it here, in my car or my classroom."

"Find what?"

"Sorry, Josh. I can't tell you."

"Why not?"

"Several reasons, Son."

"Is it...a map?"

Mr. Ladd seemed startled. "A map?"

"Like maybe to the...uh, to the place I saw in both your picture and the stranger's. The Shark Pit."

"Please! Don't say those words aloud!"

"Where is the map, Dad?"

"I didn't say it was a map."

"But whatever it is, you'll have to take it with you to Hawaii, won't you?"

"Yes, of course."

"Could the burglar try to take it *then?*"

Mr. Ladd laughed. "On a plane filled with about five hundred passengers? No, Son, I don't think so." He placed his arm around Josh's shoulder and smiled down at him in a fatherly way. "Now, you try to put this out of your mind. Concentrate on finishing the school year because nothing more is going to happen."

He was wrong. Two nights later, Mr. Ladd came home from school with upsetting news. "My classroom was broken into last night," he said grimly.

"Oh, John! No!" Mrs. Ladd exclaimed.

He nodded. "Nothing was missing, however, and damage was minimal."

"Why would anybody break into a history classroom? There's nothing to steal!"

"Dad, do you think it was the same guy who broke into our house?" Josh asked thoughtfully.

Mr. Ladd looked searchingly at his son before answering. "The police suspect juveniles, but it didn't look like that type of vandalism to me. It wasn't the same as what I've seen in other teachers' classes."

Though Josh was troubled by the break-ins and the growing mystery, he tried to fill his mind with thoughts of school ending, visiting Hawaii and seeing Tank again. He could hardly wait! Josh just hoped he could leave behind the uneasy feelings when they arrived in Hawaii.

At last, school was out for the summer and the Ladd family was aboard the giant four-engine jet plane. Josh was so excited that it seemed the nearly five-hour flight would never end. But before he knew it, the plane eased down past the volcanic landmark called Diamond Head, and delighted passengers strained to see out of the little oval windows. The plane then swung low over the beautiful blue-green Pacific Ocean, with its majestic white-capped waves rolling toward shore. The landing was smooth at Honolulu, the capital of the fiftieth state.

"We're here!" Josh cried, unbuckling his seat belt. "I can hardly wait to see Tank again!"

Josh was secretly scared that his allergy would act up when the cabin door opened and he took his first breath of Hawaiian air. If that happened, he'd made up his mind to pretend he was fine so nothing would mess up his plans to be with Tank.

It seemed there were hundreds of people getting off ahead of the Ladd family, but at last they stood at the open door. Josh glanced out at the outdoor upper-level concrete concourse. The first soft warm touch of the famous trade winds caressed his cheek. He automatically took a deep breath and glanced around.

To his left, beyond the terminal building, lush green mountains rose immediately behind the city. Josh had studied enough in preparation for coming that he knew those were called the Koolau Range*. The sky was the bluest and clearest Josh had seen in years. But it was the air that made Josh cry out.

"Hey! I can breathe!" he excitedly told his family. He again filled his lungs full of air. "I can breathe!" he repeated.

"Good for you!" Tiffany said. "Now can I get off so I can find Marsha?"

The Ladds left the plane and flowed in a human river of debarking passengers toward the terminal. The warm sun and pleasant trade winds caused everyone to hastily remove their coats. Josh tried to rush ahead, but the crowd was too densely packed. He let himself be carried with the others into the glass-walled terminal.

Above the hubbub of voices, Josh caught the smell of flowers and something sweet, like pineapple. He heard Hawaiian musicians playing ukuleles* and saw young, colorfully dressed, brown-skinned men and women rushing forward with bright flower leis* to greet some passengers.

"There they are!" Mr. Ladd cried, pointing over the crowd.

Josh saw the Catlett family pushing forward with several pretty flower leis draped over their left arms.

"Aloha*!" Mr. Catlett cried, easing through the crowd. He was as slender as a golf club. Josh had studied enough of Hawaii to recognize that Tank's father wore a white aloha shirt* with a red hibiscus* design. His pants were white. His pretty wife had on a long blue muumuu*. Marsha wore pale green shorts and a tank top. She was shorter than Tiffany, although both girls were nearly the same age.

The four adults met with glad cries, handshakes and hugs. The Catletts slipped leis over Mr. and Mrs. Ladd's heads, then over Tiffany and Nathan's. Josh was last. Tank's mother threw a fragrant, slightly damp, purple-and-white lei around his neck. He was embarrassed when she kissed him on the cheek and cried, "Aloha! Welcome to our island!"

Mr. Catlett and Marsha also eased leis over Josh's head, but he barely noticed. His eyes were on Tank who had held back until all the Ladds had flowers piled up to their chins. Then Tank stepped forward, gently removing a fragrant plumeria* lei from his tanned left forearm.

"Hi!" Tank said, slipping the garland over Josh's head. "Boy, am I glad to see you!" It was the fastest sentence Josh had ever heard from his slow-talking friend.

Tank's straight blond hair was bleached almost white from the sun. He wore a loose-fitting, yellow-and-red aloha shirt, matching shorts and sandals.

"Me, too," Josh said, wiping a drop of water off his chin from the leis.

Josh was big for his age, but Tank was bigger. At twelve, he was taller, broader in the shoulders and heavier by ten pounds than Josh. Both boys' arms and shoulders showed unusual development from a lifetime of swimming.

The two friends grinned and made small talk until the bags were loaded and the families settled into the Catletts' station wagon. As the boys crawled into the very back end with the bags, Tank asked, "The doctor let you swim yet?"

"Yes, as long as I feel okay! He wouldn't let me for a couple months after my last allergy attack, but I'm okay now."

Tank leaned closer and whispered, "I'm glad, because you'll never believe where we're going!"

"Yeah? Where?" Josh asked, automatically whispering back as he remembered the secret Tank had mentioned on the phone.

"Can't tell you here! Wait'll we're alone! But you're going to love it!"

As the station wagon pulled away from the curb, out of the corner of his eye Josh saw a man run from the terminal. Josh turned his head in time to see the well-dressed man push past other people waiting for a cab at the curb.

The man threw his bags into the cab's back seat and pointed toward the Catlett station wagon. Then the man jumped into the cab's backseat. It pulled away from the curb.

"Uh-oh!" Josh whispered to Tank.

"What?" his friend demanded.

"It's him!"

"Who are you talking about?"

"The stranger! He's followed us to Hawaii!"

Chapter Three

ESCAPE TO TROUBLE

"**W**hat stranger?" Tank demanded.

"The man in that cab!" Josh said, pointing to the vehicle about a hundred yards behind them. "I saw him back home before I knew we were coming to Hawaii!"

He wanted to tell Tank the whole story, but decided to check with his father first. Josh turned in the station wagon and raised his voice. "Dad, is it okay now to talk about. . .you know. . ."

Mr. Ladd twisted in the right front seat to look past the mothers and daughters in the backseat. "We're here in Hawaii, so why not?"

"Then he's following us!"

"Who's following us?" Mr. Ladd asked.

"Yeah, who?" chimed in Nathan, who was squeezed between his father and Mr. Catlett in the front seat.

Josh pointed to the cab which was following at a safe distance. "The stranger! The one with the pictures! I saw him run out of the terminal and get in that cab. He must've been on the same plane we were! Now he's right behind us!"

Everyone started asking questions at once, but Mr. Ladd motioned for them to be quiet. He stared out of the station wagon's rear window. "You sure, Son?

"I'm sure, Dad!"

Mr. Ladd said, "Hmmm? That's a surprise!" He turned to face Mr. Catlett. "Sam, would you mind doing me a favor? Can you turn off as soon as you can?"

"Sure, but what's going on, John?"

"I want to see if that cab is really following us."

"Why would someone—?"

"I'll explain in a minute," Mr. Ladd interrupted. "Can you turn off at the next road?"

"Sure, if it's important!"

Josh's excitement rose as Mr. Catlett suddenly took a side road and the cab followed. "He's still with us, Dad!"

Mr. Catlett glanced over Nathan's head where he was seated between the two men in the front seat. "John, you want me to take a couple more side streets to make sure?"

"I'd appreciate it, Sam!"

"Then hang on, everyone! We won't go fast, but we're about to do some twisting and turning."

"What's going on?" Mrs. Catlett asked with concern.

Mr. Ladd replied, "I'll tell all of you in a couple of minutes if he's still following us."

Josh felt a keen sense of fear from unknown dangers as the big station wagon wound in and out of side streets.

After about five minutes, while everyone got insistently more vocal to know what was going on, Mr. Ladd said, "Well, there's no doubt he is following us! Sam, would you mind not taking us to our hotel until after we lose that guy?"

"Sure thing! I'll give you a quick scenic tour. And sooner or later, he'll get caught in traffic. Then will you tell us what's going on?"

"You keep your eyes on the road, Sam, and I'll explain," Mr. Ladd said as Tank's father eased the big station wagon up steep, winding streets in a residential district.

Subconsciously, Josh was aware that most of the wooden houses had rusted corrugated metal roofs. Flowering trees and shrubs grew everywhere. Some hedges were beefsteak red and strangely beautiful.

Mr. Ladd raised his voice so everyone could hear. "I'm on a confidential article assignment for a history magazine, and apparently somebody else is trying to follow me."

"But why?" Mrs. Catlett asked anxiously from the backseat. "Could it have anything to do with the burglary Josh wrote Tank about?"

"I don't really know, Barbara. Josh, tell them what you know about the stranger."

With mounting excitement, the boy told about meeting the stranger and the two pictures. Josh started to mention that his father had later showed him the same photograph and almost said something about the Shark Pit, but Mr. Ladd broke in.

"That's enough for now, Son! Thanks!"

Mr. Catlett had swung back onto a highway that led up into the Koolau Range behind Honolulu. The cab fell farther and farther behind in traffic.

The passengers were filled with questions. Mr. Ladd twisted in the front seat to answer. "I don't know who he is, or why he's following me. But it obviously has something to do with my assignment. My guess is that he may also have a lead on where I'm going, but he's missing something. Anyway, I don't see how it could be dangerous."

"What could he be missing?" Nathan asked.

"Well, maybe he knows *what* I'm after, but he doesn't know *where* it is. So he's trying to follow me there."

"To the place in the photograph?" Tank guessed.

"Maybe," Mr. Ladd admitted.

"But why, Sam?" Mrs. Catlett asked.

Mr. Ladd shrugged. "I thought I was on an exclusive assignment, but the editor warned me somebody else might have gotten wind of the discovery and...."

"Discovery?" Josh interrupted. "What kind of discovery?"

"I'm sorry, but I can't say."

Tiffany cried, "Oh, I know! It's some famous historic thing, isn't it, Dad?"

Mrs. Ladd reminded her daughter, "Your father just

said he can't say what it is!"

Tank asked, "Do you know where it is...I mean, the place in the picture Josh saw?"

"I have a map," Mr. Ladd answered.

Josh felt his heart jump. So there was a map! But of what?

Tank lowered his voice so only Josh could hear. "I've got a map, too."

"Yeah? Of what?"

"Shh! Not now!"

Josh was frustrated but sighed and watched the road and scenery fall away behind the station wagon as it climbed high above the city. The cab could no longer be seen, though there was no question that it was still following their car. Through the rear window, Honolulu sprawled below and Pearl Harbor's waters looked like melted silver. From here, it was easy to see how the ancient center of Diamond Head's volcano had caved in.

As the vehicle rounded another curve, still climbing, Josh exclaimed, "Hey! That looks like the rain forests we see on the educational channel!"

"It is!" Mr. Catlett replied, bringing the station wagon around a curve and into the dense shade of the trees. "This is semitropical country, you know. Hang on, everyone! After we round this next curve, I'm going to pull off and stop on a side road!"

After they were into the curve where anyone following could not see, Mr. Catlett slowed and turned off onto a dirt road. He explained, "This is so overgrown with trailing vines and dense foliage that unless you knew it was here, you'd drive right by and not see it. Let's hope that happens to the guy following us!"

Tank's father parked and cut the engine. Josh was aware of how quiet it was. Every breath was held and nobody moved as each eye strained to see what would happen.

Josh's heart was thumping loudly. He wondered what they'd do if the stranger found them now?

The station wagon rested in the deep shadows of dense overhead branches. Long vines trailed down to the ground. It was like being in a mountainous jungle with a highway going through it, Josh thought.

A couple of minutes later, Josh cried out, "There he goes!"

From the front seat, Mr. Ladd gave a big sigh. "Thanks, Sam! Great driving! Now, let's get to our hotel."

Mr. Catlett said, "He'll end up on the windward* side, but we'll turn around and drive back to Waikiki. We'll take you by our apartment so you can see where we live. It's right on the way to your hotel."

As the station wagon eased back down the mountains toward Honolulu, Josh and Tank tried to talk their parents into letting the boys spend the night together. Tiffany and Marsha wanted to do the same, but Mrs. Catlett said their apartment was simply too small. They'd have plenty of time to talk tomorrow, she said.

Josh was feeling frustrated, but he tried to listen to Mr. Catlett's description of the area as they drove along Waikiki Beach and then turned left immediately under Diamond Head.

"That's where we live!" Tank exclaimed, pointing. "Right beneath the shadow of this old volcano."

As Mr. Catlett eased the station wagon into a parking area behind the apartments, Josh watched white pigeons or doves flying high above Diamond Head and then settling in front of small holes near the top.

"Oh, there's Roger Okamoto and his parents!" Tank said. "Roger lives in the same apartments with us. He knows lots of neat places to go snorkeling* and stuff."

Mr. Catlett stopped the station wagon. "You'll all like the Okamotos! They're third-generation Japanese-Americans whose ancestors came here to work the cane and pine plantations."

"Cane? Pine?" Nathan asked.

"Sugar cane and pineapple!" Tiffany explained. "Don't you remember us reading about that while we were getting ready to visit Hawaii?"

"Uh...sure!" Nathan answered. "I just wanted to see if you knew."

"Little brothers!" Tiffany muttered.

Josh studied the family approaching the station wagon. Roger Okamoto looked about a year older than Josh and Tank, and wore faded blue cutoffs and sandals with no shirt. He was very slender, with copper tan skin and intensely black hair that stuck out above his ears.

Mr. Okamoto was stocky, with traces of gray in his dark hair. He greeted the Catletts and then acknowledged the introduction to the Ladd family.

"Aloha, and welcome to Hawaii," Mr. Okamoto said with a big grin. "If we had known you were going to drive by, we'd have had leis for all of you."

"We're already buried in them," Mr. Ladd said with a chuckle, flipping the leis around his chin. "But thanks for the thought."

Josh noticed that Mr. Okamoto was a strongly built man of average height, with a wide, friendly smile. He wore casual pants and a white aloha shirt decorated with coral-colored seashells.

His wife was shorter, with closely cropped black hair. She wore a loose-fitting, blue-and-white muumuu. "We have heard so much about you," Mrs. Okamoto said. "You must come for dinner soon."

Josh's father and mother agreed they'd love to do that. Roger stuck his head in the back window between Josh and Tank. "Hi, Bruddah!" he greeted Josh.

"Hi," Josh replied, glancing uncertainly at Tank. Josh detected an accent in each of the Okamotos. Their voices tended to go up at the end of sentences, somewhat like when a question was asked.

Tank explained, "Kids around here usually use some of the local Pidgin English*, like 'Bruddah,' which means Brother."

Josh nodded and started to say something, but Roger turned to Tank.

"Now that your friend is here, you ready to go check out that map?"

"Shh!" Tank warned. "Not so loud!"

"Not to worry! Parents never believe kids have anything like a treasure map!"

Josh frowned. "A treasure—?"

"Later!" Tank interrupted.

Josh was a little annoyed at not being able to learn what was going on. And how come Roger knew about a map if it was so secret?

When everyone had said goodbye, Mr. Catlett drove the station wagon back down the hill toward the ocean. The boys helped get the baggage up to the Ladds' three rooms in a small hotel a few blocks off the famous Waikiki Beach.

"Tank, when can we talk?" Josh asked quietly as the boys followed the others back to the station wagon.

"Tomorrow, I hope."

"What about Roger? Where's he fit in?"

"Shh! Not now! I'll tell you everything at church tomorrow! Pretty soon, we're going on an adventure you'll never forget!"

Chapter Four

A SUNDAY SURPRISE

The next morning, Josh opened his eyes to see a flower lei draped across the headboard on his bed. He remembered Mrs. Catlett had explained it was customary for first-time visitors to Hawaii to do that. The fragrance from the string of flowers was almost over-poweringly sweet.

Josh threw back the single sheet he'd used for a cover. "Right after church," Tank had said. "What was he talking about?" Josh asked himself. "And what's Roger got to do with the map and Tank's big secret? Well, I'll soon find out."

Josh glanced at his brother's nearby twin bed. It was empty, the single sheet used for a cover was turned back. The light was on in the bathroom.

"Nathan?" Josh called.

There was no answer. Wearing only shortie pajama bottoms he'd brought along, Josh rapidly crossed to the bathroom. His little brother's pajamas and underclothes were scattered all around.

Josh jerked the tub's shower curtain aside, but Nathan wasn't there. "I should have known," Josh told himself as he left the bathroom. "He wouldn't take a bath without somebody making him do it."

For a moment, Josh remembered the stranger and had a horrible feeling that somehow he had found them and had taken Nathan. Then Josh's eyes flickered to the motel room's front door. The security chain had been released and hung down. Josh sighed with relief. "Probably gone to see Mom and Dad."

Still feeling a little jittery, Josh slowly looked around the room. Brilliant sunshine from a flawless blue sky poured through the window pane. There were louvers under the window to permit the trade winds to pass through the room and out similar louvers on the opposite wall. The breezes lightly brushed Josh's bare chest with a gentle, almost unfelt touch.

Through the window, Josh saw palm tree fronds rattling in the trade winds. Directly under the fronds, coconuts were growing. Surprisingly, the nuts were almost a pumpkin color.

Josh heard birds cooing and turned around. The sound came through a screen door on the opposite side of the small motel room. He eased up to it, trying to spot the birds outside.

They stirred at his approach, but didn't fly. He stopped and watched through the screen. They looked much like the familiar doves in California, except these had dark stripes and were smaller. They cooed differently, too, but they were definitely doves, he decided. He concluded that these must be the small, barred Japanese doves he'd read about in preparation for coming to Hawaii.

Nathan opened the outside door. He was very neat in a light summer suit with a tie that his mother always insisted he wear. "How come you're not dressed? We're all ready for Sunday school!"

"Be ready in no time!" Josh replied, heading for the shower.

When Mr. Catlett turned the big station wagon into the church parking lot half an hour later, Josh was surprised. "Hey!" he cried, pointing through the back window, "those walls don't go all the way to the roof!"

Mr. Catlett laughed as he carefully guided the station wagon through neatly but informally dressed people of many racial backgrounds. "That's true, Josh! That's deliberate so we can use nature's air conditioning system! The trade winds go over the top of the walls and circulate across the congregation before moving on out the other side!"

"Don't crooks crawl over the tops of those walls and steal things at night?"

"No, not so far," Mr. Catlett replied. "Well, let's get out and I'll introduce you around."

Josh felt out of place with his usual church suit and tie. Apparently his parents did, too. They laughed and remarked that next time Mr. Ladd and the boys would wear pants and casual aloha shirts like the local worshippers. Mrs. Ladd and Marsha would don cotton dresses similar to what other women and girls had on.

As the two families walked across the parking lot, Josh glanced around. The Koolaus rose behind him, ragged and sharply pointed, unlike the mountains around Los Angeles. In the other direction, past the church, he could glimpse the Pacific Ocean.

The church grounds were an explosion of flowers and shrubs. The gray trunks of the royal palm trees contrasted with the hibiscus, which grew everywhere in yellow, red and other colors. These were mixed with heavy clusters of coral, white and purple bougainvillea*. Josh had thought Southern California had lots of flowers, but they were nothing compared to what grew here.

The Catletts introduced a number of smiling parishioners walking across the parking lot. Josh caught Chinese, Japanese, Okinawan, Hawaiian, and other surnames. He couldn't remember any of them.

"Tank, where's Roger?" Josh asked as the two families approached the church building.

"He won't be here; he's a Buddhist*."

"He is? I've never met one before."

Josh was interested in what people believed, so he wanted to ask more. However, he focused his attention on a slight man in black robes and bifocals who greeted the two families at the outside church doors.

Mr. Catlett said, "Dr. Chin, I'd like you to meet our

good friends from the mainland, John and Mary Ladd, and their children: Tiffany, Josh and Nathan."

"Aloha and welcome to the Lord's house!" Dr. Chin said with a broad smile. He shook hands with everyone as Mr. Catlett explained that Dr. Chin was of Chinese descent and served as pastor of the church.

That news made Josh thoughtful. Josh studied him a little more closely. At home, the Ladd family were long-time members of a church where the minister was white and always wore a suit, but never robes. Dr. Chin's salt-and-pepper hair was cut rather short and seemed to be combed from the ears back to the center. It seemed to make a ridge in the middle of his head.

"He's a great pastor," Mrs. Catlett assured the Ladds as they headed toward the church office to register the children for Sunday school. "You'll love him!"

Tank grinned. "Especially when he comes to visit and takes off his shoes outside the door!"

"You're kidding!" Josh exclaimed.

"Nope! But you'll do the same when you go to his house!"

"Or ours," Mrs. Catlett added. "That's a great custom many of us have adopted here. So is singing the doxology* in eight languages. We change week by week, but you're in luck—this week it's English!"

When the family split up to attend Sunday school classes, Josh followed Tank into a small side room filled with boys and girls—but not one was Caucasian*.

Everyone was friendly, but Josh was keenly aware that all of the others, including the teacher, had dark skin.

Josh hoped for an opportunity to ask Tank about the "treasure" map, but the teacher came in and started the lesson. He was a small Filipino who said the lesson was on obedience to parents. Josh barely listened to the various scriptural references because everything was so strange, and he desperately wanted to know about the treasure map.

That opportunity came in the break between Sunday school and church. "Look, Tank," Josh said when they'd stepped outside the building into the bright sunshine, "Let's skip the punch and cookies and talking with everybody! Let's talk about important things!"

Tank lowered his voice. "You mean the map?"

Josh nodded and almost whispered. "Yes, and Roger. How come he knows about the map when you couldn't tell me?"

Tank led Josh across the parking lot away from the church. "Well, because he was with me when the old Hawaiian gave it to me."

"What Hawaiian? Why'd he give it to you?"

Tank began in his slow, easy-speaking manner that sometimes drove Josh crazy. "One day Roger and I were out exploring one of those little pocket valleys. They're all around these mountains." Tank waved toward the Koolaus.

Josh looked up into the range where Tank pointed. He

saw many small valleys an acre or two across that had been formed by the ancient lava flows trailing down the range.

Tank continued, "Roger and I came to this old house which sat all alone, at the edge of the jungle. It was about to fall down and had a rusty tin roof. Wasn't much to look at. We thought it was empty and started to explore it.

"Then we heard someone calling and went to look. It turned out to be an old Hawaiian man. He was big, like many Hawaiians are. But he was sick and barely alive. Roger and I went for help, which was no big deal. But when he got well, he sent his grandson to find us."

Tank paused, and Josh prompted him to continue.

"The grandson—about our age—took us to see the old man who was then up and around in his little house. He said he didn't have anything to give us, but suggested that maybe we'd like an old map."

Josh felt his breathing start to speed up. "The map! What's the treasure?"

Tank shrugged and continued in his slow way. "He wouldn't say exactly what it is. Said it's supposed to be something very valuable to his people—an ancient Hawaiian treasure. He said he accidentally found the place when he was a boy. Told us he was scared because of the kapu* sticks...but he took a quick look, then got out fast."

"Kapu sticks?"

"Means taboo, forbidden or keep out in Hawaiian.

Anyway, he took a quick look, but the kapu sticks meant it was something he wasn't supposed to see. So he left fast and never returned."

Except for the kapu or forbidden element, which spelled excitement and danger to Josh, he was disappointed. "What kind of treasure could it be?" Josh asked. "And if it's so valuable, why didn't he give it to his grandson?"

"I told you. It's kapu to them."

"Where'd he get the map?"

"Some years after he'd been to the cave, he drew the map and kept it all those years."

Josh's eyes widened with interest. "Cave?"

"There are lots of caves, or burial chambers, around here. The old Hawaiians used to bury the bones of their chiefs in them."

"You got the map with you?"

"No."

Josh was really disappointed, but Tank seemed not to notice. He continued, "The grandson said he had made photocopies a year or so before, just in case the old man lost the original. But the one that the old man gave us looked very old to Roger and me. So we think it's genuine."

"You mean that's all there is to it?"

"Isn't that enough? We've got a reason to go exploring to check out that map! Won't that be fun?"

For a moment, Josh hesitated. "I suppose it would.

When can we start?"

"Soon as we can get to Maui."

"Maui? Isn't that another of the Hawaiian islands?"

"Right. Maui is a neighboring island to Oahu, where we are now. So we've got to find a way to fly over."

Josh's excitement began to return as he tried to think what the treasure might be. Maybe black pearls or something rare from under the sea. To find out, they had to somehow get to Maui.

At lunch, an unexpected opportunity came to do that. The Catletts took the Ladd family to a downtown Honolulu restaurant. The walls were only about four feet tall, and the two families were seated at a table where Josh could reach across the wall and touch the ti*, banana* and other plants growing there.

As the meal started, Mr. Catlett explained that locals always ate with chopsticks. Visitors (never called tourists) ate with *"haole chopsticks,"* meaning a fork.

The Ladd children were all disappointed that instead of the familiar potatoes, rice was automatically served with all dishes. Still, in the spirit of adventure, they tried the local favorites.

During the meal, Mr. Ladd said, "Well, I guess that tomorrow I can fly on over to Maui and begin my assignment."

"Maui?" Josh exclaimed, lowering the chopsticks he was trying to use for the first time. "Can Tank and I go with you? Huh, Dad? And maybe Roger?"

Before Mr. Ladd could answer, Tiffany chimed in, "How about me and Marsha?"

Nathan sputtered through a mouthful of rice, "And me?"

A lively discussion followed. Finally, Mr. Catlett offered a suggestion. "I have an important supplier who owns a small ocean-front hotel. He's said we may use the rooms any time, so...suppose the two mothers go and take all the kids?"

Mr. Ladd had to wait until the approving cries of the children subsided. Then they worked out the details. Nathan would be allowed to go snorkeling with Mr. and Mrs. Ladd at the hotel's beach. Mr. Ladd would take the older children with him to a certain point.

"My assignment is such that I can't take you all the way," he said. "But you can come part of the way." He concluded, "You wait for me there and I'll go on alone. Everyone must do exactly what I say, okay?"

"Okay!" The word seemed to come from all the kids at once.

After lunch, the Catletts dropped the Ladds off at their Honolulu hotel. As Mr. Ladd topped the stairs to their second story rooms, he cried, "Uh-oh! Mary, we left the door open to our room!"

"No, we didn't! I distinctly remember locking it!"

The family rushed into the room and stopped in shock. Mrs. Ladd exclaimed, "Oh, no! Not again!"

Josh saw everything had been scattered about, like

when their home had been burglarized. His skin tingled with goosebumps. The stranger! It had to be him!

Mrs. Ladd ran to the telephone while her husband rushed into the closet. Josh was still looking at the mess in disbelief when Mr. Ladd reappeared from the closet. His face was grim.

"My map—it's gone!"

Chapter Five

CHASING AFTER SHADOWS

When the Hawaiian police had come and gone, Mrs. Ladd phoned the Catletts. She told them about the burglary, and they said they'd be right over. While the Ladds waited, the mother began picking up the mess the intruder had made. Automatically, her family helped. They were silently thinking of all they'd heard their father tell the authorities.

"Dad, I still can't figure out how that man—whoever he is—found us," Josh said as he righted a dresser drawer that had been dumped upside down on the floor. "I thought Mr. Catlett had lost him forever in traffic."

Mr. Ladd knelt to pull some of his shirts from where they'd been partially thrown under the bed. Nathan placed them on top of the bed. Mr. Ladd said, "I don't know either, Son. But his getting that map sure hurts us all."

Josh paused, sensing something important in his father's quiet words. "You mean because you can't find the place to get the story for the editor?"

"More than that, Josh. There's something I haven't told

any of you kids."

"What's that?" Tiffany asked, coming out of the closet where she'd rehung her father's slacks.

"Remember back in California when I first told you about coming to Hawaii and said there was something that was secret?"

All three children solemnly nodded.

"I've been thinking of buying a weekly newspaper here and moving our whole family to Hawaii to live."

Josh's mouth fell open in surprise. "Move here permanently?"

His father nodded. All three kids broke into exclamations, but their father held up his hand.

"Not so fast! Without that map and the article for the editor, there'll be no money to buy a newspaper, so we certainly can't move here!"

Josh and Tiffany groaned in disappointment, but not Nathan. "I don't think I want to move to Hawaii," he announced. "Mom and Dad have Mr. and Mrs. Catlett, Josh and Tiffany have Tank and Marsha, but I don't have anybody."

Josh turned to encourage his little brother just as the Catletts arrived. "Hey, everybody," Josh shouted instead, "We may move to Hawaii!"

Mr. Ladd raised his voice. "Son, I told you—!"

"We'll find a way!" Josh interrupted. "We've got to!"

There was an excited buzz from everyone as the Catletts were briefly told about the burglary, the Ladds' plans to move to Hawaii, and the stolen map that threatened those plans.

Josh quickly motioned his best friend outside the sliding screen door onto the small lanai* where they could talk privately. Josh teetered between bursting with happiness at the possibility of moving to Hawaii, and utter discouragement, knowing they couldn't unless the stranger or the map were found.

"Your father must have looked at the map often enough to get a pretty good idea of where the place is," Tank said. "Maybe he can find it without the map."

Josh's eyes lit up. "Yeah, maybe he can! Let's ask!"

As the boys turned toward the screen door, Josh thought of something. He lowered his voice. "Did you bring our map with you?"

"You kidding? When your mother called about the burglary, we dropped everything and came right over!"

"When can I see the map?"

"I'll bring it the next time we meet."

As the boys re-entered the bedroom, Tank's father was sitting on the one big upholstered chair. "Let's see if I've got this straight, John. The magazine editor gave you a map to a remote area on Maui's coastline; a place called the Shark Pit!"

Tank exclaimed, "The Shark Pit? Is it called that because of what I think it means?"

Mr. Ladd shrugged. "I don't know how it got its name. But it doesn't matter, because I was going to go overland,

and not by the ocean side."

Josh broke in with the question he and Tank had been discussing. "Dad, can you find the place without the map?"

"I've looked at it so often I have a pretty good idea of how to get there."

Josh felt his heart thump with hope. "Then why don't you do it?"

Tiffany spoke up. "But Dad, even if you do remember, now that the stranger has the map, it'll be easy for him to beat you there!"

Mr. Ladd nodded solemnly. "Unfortunately, that's true."

Nathan asked, "What's there—a pirate's treasure or something?"

Mr. Ladd ruffled his youngest son's hair. "Nothing so romantic as that! My editor didn't know what it was exactly, but it's supposed to be some kind of priceless historical artifact."

Josh shrugged. That didn't interest him, but he could understand why a history teacher might like it.

"What's that mean?" questioned Nathan.

"Artifact?" Mr. Ladd asked. "Oh, that's something man-made, and historical means something from past events, like a long time ago when something happened."

Nathan said, "I knew that!"

Tiffany groaned in exasperation. "Then why'd you ask? Little brothers! Sometimes—"

"Tiffany!" her mother interrupted. "Your father hasn't finished."

Mr. Ladd continued, "Well, the 'priceless' part means this thing—whatever it is—is so rare that it's worth more than money could buy. At least, to the Hawaiians."

"You mean, like to a museum, dear?" Mrs. Ladd asked.

Mr. Ladd nodded.

"Well," Josh said, "it's sure important to us, too! No matter what it is! Dad, we've got to get it back, somehow!"

His father sighed. "I want to, Son. But there are surely a lot of obstacles in the way!"

An idea hit Josh. He snapped his fingers and his heart sped up with hope of how they might get to stay in Hawaii. "Dad, you said you sort of remember the map. Enough to get close, anyway. Right?"

"I think so."

"Then we've still got a chance! Maybe you could beat him there!"

"Son, you're forgetting that I don't know what he looks like. Only you've seen him, so he could walk right by me and I wouldn't know who he was."

"I could go with you!"

"Hmmm?" Mr. Ladd frowned, looking down at Josh in sudden thought. "Yes, I suppose that might work."

"Then let's do it!" Josh cried.

"Let me go, too!" Tank shouted. "I could help!"

Tiffany added, "And me! Marsha and I could help, too!"

Mr. Ladd held up both hands to stop the rising cries of excitement. "Hold on, everybody! I'm not going to risk anybody's safety! I don't think the stranger's dangerous. He's more of a coward, I'd guess, because he's never faced me, but only burglarized us when nobody was around. "But I'm not going to take any chances! After all, he really wanted that map! So who knows what he'd be like if he were cornered? Besides, the last thing I need is a bunch of kids to watch out for while I'm trying to catch a crook!"

Josh spoke quickly. "But since you'll need me to identify him, can Tank come along?"

"Sorry, Josh, but I can't risk that."

Mr. Catlett spoke up. "John, it might be wise to have someone else along. I'd go, but I'm absolutely swamped at work. But since this stranger's apparently not dangerous, Tank could go."

Tank exclaimed, "Thanks, Dad!"

Tiffany groaned. "That's not fair! Why can't Marsha and I go, too?"

Mr. Catlett cleared his throat. "Why don't I call my supplier and see if he can provide lodging for all of you at Lahaina? Then John can decide who goes with him while the others stay and enjoy themselves at the hotel. You can rent snorkeling gear, masks and fins there."

A happy chorus of approval erupted from the older

children.

Mr. Ladd cautioned, "Remember, even if I allow some of you to go with me, you can only go part way. Then I'll leave you behind at a given point while I go on alone. You older kids can have fun inside the reef until I return. Agreed?"

Tank, Tiffany and Marsha eagerly agreed, but Josh was worried. "Dad, I've got to go all the way with you so you'll recognize the stranger if you run into him. Besides, it could be dangerous for you to go by yourself."

Mr. Ladd was firm. "I'll take you only as far as I think it's safe. If we haven't run into him by then, I think it's fair to assume he's gotten there ahead of us and left. But I've got to see the place for myself and see if I can figure out what was so important."

He concluded by saying those were his conditions. If they were accepted, everyone had better do some quick packing so they could catch a late flight to Maui. Everyone agreed, and soon they were all on their way to the airport.

There, the two families ran into the Okamotos who had just seen a friend off to Japan. Roger talked his parents into letting him go along to Maui.

On the short jet flight to the neighboring island, Josh and Tank filled Roger in on everything. They landed at Kahalui where Mr. Ladd rented a big station wagon. They drove to the old whaling port of Lahaina where Mr. Catlett had made arrangements for everyone to spend the night.

It was a pretty place right on the ocean. There was one large hotel facing the beach. Many small individual cabins resembling little grass shacks were scattered over a grassy area. The four boys shared a cabin that had two sets of bunk beds.

Roger, as the most experienced swimmer, went with Mr. Ladd and Nathan to rent equipment at the hotel. The two mothers and two sisters strolled around the grounds while Josh and Tank got settled.

Josh examined a framed color map of Maui on the wall of their cabin. The island vaguely resembled a woman's head, neck and upper body. "You know, Tank, I just can't believe you didn't have time to bring our treasure map."

"Wouldn't help," Tank said, walking up to stand beside Josh. Tank pointed to the shoreline on the woman's head. "We're over here at Lahaina and the map showed the treasure is way off over that way!" He ran his finger along the map, past the island's neck to the ocean below Haleakala Crater*, the world's largest dormant volcano.

"We're so close and yet so far!" Josh moaned, looking at the map where mountain ridges ran from more than ten thousand feet high right into the ocean. "Can either you or Roger remember anything about the map?"

"Some," Tank admitted. He studied the wall map closely. "It's below Haleakala. Highway 31 runs along here, along the ocean. See? Off the coast here is Molokini Island. That's on our map. So as I remember our map, the treasure is somewhere around here, right on the ocean."

"Sure looks like rugged country!" Josh said in awe. "The rest of the island is pretty well developed, but this area looks wild! Maybe it's because these ridges are old lava flows. See? The map shows they go right down to the ocean. I wish Dad would give us some hint where his map showed...Listen! What's that?"

"Conch shell*," Tank said, stepping to the window. "They're blowing it to let visitors know it's time for sunset torch-lighting ceremonies. Come on, you malihini!* Let's go see!"

As the boys ran out of their cabin, Josh saw his father, mother and sister leave the hotel with Tank's mother and sister. Roger wasn't with them. Josh turned to see a power-fully built young Hawaiian, his brown chest and forearms bare, remove the huge seashell from his lips.

The two families sat together on a bench with an unobstructed view of the beach and ocean. The sun was sinking rapidly below the horizon. Josh had studied enough of the old roadstead anchorage* to recognize the small island of Lanai ahead of them.

"Just think!" Mr. Ladd said, "This great open expanse of ocean in front of us was once filled with whaling ships. What troubles those whalermen gave the missionaries who started coming here in 1820!"

"Oh, look!" Mrs. Ladd exclaimed, pointing. "They're lighting the tiki torches*!"

In the distance, Josh saw a bare-chested Hawaiian youth wearing a loincloth start running toward them. He swung a flaming torch, which fluttered in the trade winds. He slowed slightly as he came to the first tiki torch. He swung the flame up and the torch leaped to life. Then he ran to the next, and on until every one was lit and the flames danced with life.

Hawaiian musicians dressed in colorful costumes began playing their ukuleles in the distinct Hawaiian style just as Roger jogged up. He was loaded down with rented fins, snorkels and face masks. "This is good equipment," he said to Josh. "I examined it all." Josh noticed that Roger was not speaking the hard-to-understand Pidgin English that he often used. He now sounded no different from Josh himself.

When the lighting ceremony was over, everyone went to dinner and then headed for their rooms. Josh's chest didn't hurt. He could breathe freely. His allergy wasn't bothering him. He was determined to move to Hawaii, but that meant that tomorrow they had to beat the stranger to the treasure—if it wasn't too late.

That knowledge made it hard for Josh to sleep. He finally dozed off, but awakened in the middle of the night. The musicians had long since finished playing. There was no sound except the flame of the tiki torch whispering in the wind.

As Josh stared silently at the darkened ceiling, thinking, a reckless idea leaped into his mind. He sat up abruptly.

"Even though Dad said we can only go part way, I'm not going to do it! I'll follow him!"

Josh lay down again, but couldn't sleep. He tried not to think of what possible danger might result from his disobedience.

Chapter Six

RACE WITH A GHOST

The next morning, Josh, Tank and Roger were already up and dressed when Mr. Ladd knocked at their door. Josh vowed not to say anything about his decision to follow his father, no matter what.

They loaded all the swimming gear into the back of the station wagon. The boys climbed into the rear seat with Josh in the middle. Tiffany and Marsha rode in front with Mr. Ladd. Mr. Ladd drove along the ocean. It was too early for the kids to be very talkative. They rode in silence past cane and pineapple fields. Once Josh watched a crop-dusting biplane flying inches above the ground, spraying to control weeds or insects in the pineapple fields.

The quiet mood evaporated when Tank leaned over and whispered to Josh, "Look at this map of Maui the rental company gave us. We're headed toward Haleakala!"

At first, the meaning was lost on Josh. He glanced at the road map where Tank's finger was following the station wagon's progress, then at the ten-thousand-foot-high Haleakala volcano outside. Josh raised his eyes to the mountain. It's crater-top was wrapped in clouds. Josh asked in disbelief, "You mean—we're going toward the place on the map the old Hawaiian gave you?"

"Sure t'ing, Bruddah!" Roger said softly.

The boys sat up and tried to control their excitement as the station wagon continued along the coast in the shadow of the great volcano. They were nearing the ancient lava flows and some of the most stark, strange country Josh had ever seen.

Mr. Ladd turned off on a dirt road that was pitted and rutted. Josh thought it didn't deserve to be called a road at all. It made the station wagon bounce and sway as it headed into a dense, jungle-like area.

Tank leaned over and whispered to Josh, "See that little thing out in the ocean that looks like a slice of watermelon rind? That's Molokini Island."

Roger grinned and said in a husky whisper. "That's on our map, too! So far, so good, Bruddahs!"

"We're really getting close to the place on our map?" Josh asked.

Tank and Roger nodded. The boys watched anxiously as the station wagon bumped slowly across the very roughest unpaved road Josh had ever seen. His father muttered, "Wish I'd rented a four-wheeled vehicle! This car wasn't made for roads like this!"

As Josh's head was snapped back and forth, he told Tank and Roger, "One thing for sure—if the stranger also went this way, he's not making much time. Maybe we can catch up to him!"

The violent rocking, swaying motion of the big vehicle made the two girls sit up. They took more interest as Mr. Ladd approached a tiny country store in a remote jungle-like area. The store's tin roof was badly rusted and the wooden front porch sagged. Mr. Ladd stopped and said, "You kids can go in and look around, but I want to speak privately to the owner."

The children agreed. Mr. Ladd approached the Oriental proprietor. Josh heard his father asking directions to a certain point.

"Ah! You, too!" the small man said with a big smile.

Josh turned around to watch as Mr. Ladd said, "I don't understand."

"You second person this morning ask same question." His voice had a slightly sing-song lilt to it.

Josh took a quick step toward the proprietor and asked, "Did he wear sunglasses that went around his eyes like this?" Josh quickly demonstrated. "Maybe wore a funny hat?"

"Ah, yesss! Same!"

Mr. Ladd asked quietly, "How long ago?"

The man smiled and shrugged. "Maybe so half-hour; maybe so more."

"Which way?" Mr. Ladd asked.

"Same way you want." The owner pointed and gave directions. When he had finished, Mr. Ladd motioned his passengers to hurry back to the station wagon. Only when they were inside and the doors closed did Josh realize how fast his heart was beating.

"Dad, the stranger's not very far ahead of us! Maybe we really do still have a chance to catch up with him—or even beat him there!"

"Let's hope you're right, Josh! If he had any troubles that delayed him, we could come up on him unexpectedly. Everyone please keep a sharp eye out! We've got about another minute or so in this bouncing vehicle, then we walk."

"Or run," Josh said, feeling the excitement grow inside him.

Roger was always shy and rarely spoke around girls, but he whispered to the boys in the backseat, "The race is on, huh, Bruddah?"

"Sure is!" Tank agreed as the wagon bounced through a narrow opening of semitropical rain forest. "Except it's like racing a ghost because nobody's seen this guy except you, Josh."

They had gone about a quarter-mile when the terrible bouncing finally stopped. Mr. Ladd steered the big vehicle off the side of the miserable excuse for a road. "Everybody out! Grab your things! We walk from here!"

They were close enough to see the ocean below them, past rugged, almost straight-down terrain. Josh was having trouble breathing, but not from his allergy. That hadn't bothered him since landing in Hawaii. His breathing problem now was from anticipation of what might be about to happen.

"If we beat the stranger," he told himself, "We can live here forever! I mean, *when* we beat the stranger!"

His heart thumping rapidly, Josh helped unload the rented snorkels, masks and fins from the wagon. Mr. Ladd opened a small flight bag and checked several items, including a camera, notepad and a long length of red rope.

Josh asked, "What's the rope for?"

"Life insurance, Son." Mr. Ladd replied. "It's nylon, like mountain climbers use. It's strong enough to lower me, if necessary. Or I can use it if I'm in brush so thick I couldn't find my way back without playing it out behind me. Okay, if you've got your gear, let's go!"

He led the way on foot through the dense, jungle-like growth toward the ocean. The five kids scrambled across ancient volcanic flows that made strange clinking sounds under their shoes.

Mr. Ladd said, "Reminds me somewhat of the sound cinder clinkers made in the furnace back East when I was a little boy."

Josh's eyes darted ceaselessly about. Could the stranger have heard them coming and hidden to attack them? He surely wouldn't have had time to get to wherever he was going and return. Josh raised his voice slightly. "Watch out we don't get ambushed."

Tiffany and Marsha giggled at the idea, but the three

boys and Mr. Ladd walked more quietly and stayed very alert. The green vegetation gave way to dry brush which Roger explained was kiawe*, or algaroba tree. It grew about as high as a house and had terrible thorns.

Suddenly, Josh caught a flash of movement as they passed a small open space. "What's that?" he asked, pointing to the small animal that had stopped and was watching them.

"Mongoose," Roger answered. "And see that red bird over there? Cardinals imported from the East."

Tiffany whispered, "Oh, how beautiful!"

"Keep your voices down, please," Mr. Ladd cautioned. He continued in a stage whisper. "Keep moving while I tell you the history of how those creatures came to these islands."

Since Josh could remember, his father had always explained about the history of things. Josh was now concerned about the stranger and too curious about the old Hawaiian's map to pay any attention to his father's quiet explanation. The girls were trying to listen, but were having trouble keeping their swimming gear from getting snagged on every bush or tree they passed.

Tiffany released her fins from a branch and asked, "What's that funny-looking open space over there?"

Her father answered, "Heiau*. I've never seen one, but that's what it has to be. Right, Roger?"

"Yes," the island boy replied shortly, as he usually did when girls were around.

Josh asked, "What's a hay-ow?"

Mr. Ladd turned around in the trail. "Ancient pagan temple grounds where the Hawaiians held religious services. They had many gods, including a shark god."

"Shark?" Tiffany repeated with a shiver.

"Oh, what's that over there?" Marsha asked, pointing off to the right where the brush was very high and dense.

"Looks like the top of an old church steeple," Mr. Ladd answered. "The missionaries built them all over these islands after they started coming here in 1820."

Josh was anxious to move on, but the girls wanted to rest a moment at the old church. They entered through a low stone fence that Mr. Ladd said was probably made of coral cut from under the sea by early Hawaiian Christians.

The church was a sad, lonely sight. The tiny abandoned wooden building sagged heavily. Yet it was beautified by several colors of bougainvillea that still grew wild from the bell tower and eaves. Very old gravestones were partially covered by fragrant plumeria and wild vanda orchids. The girls gathered a few orchids for their hair before the troop again headed down toward the sea.

Every step made Josh more uneasy. This would be an easy place for the stranger to surprise and attack them. Of course, it would be six to one against him, but not if the stranger had a weapon.

As they eased down a narrow, almost invisible trail through the brush, Josh noticed Roger looking around and dropping behind. Josh lightly touched Tank's arm and motioned for him to turn back to Roger.

"What's the matter?" Josh asked, approaching Roger.

Roger's dark eyes were bright with emotion. He whispered, "Stop behind that plumeria and I'll show you."

The boys did so. They were well protected by the large, spreading plant, although the sweet fragrance of the blossoms almost overpowered Josh's nostrils. Roger reached into his hip pocket. He pulled out a piece of paper and unfolded it.

"Hey!" Tank whispered in surprise, "That's our map!"

"Photocopy," Roger corrected him.

Tank sputtered, "You've been carrying a copy of our secret map around?"

Roger nodded. "Good thing, too!"

Tank whispered fiercely, "You know how dangerous that could be? Suppose you lost it?"

Roger shrugged. "You want to get huhu* or you want to see what I'm seeing?"

Josh said, "Tank, earlier we were wishing you'd brought the map. So let's have a look." He took hold of one side of the map as Roger unfolded it.

It only took a glance to identify Haleakala behind, the Pacific below, the heiau and church they'd just passed. The map's focal point was right at the shore. Josh asked, "What are those strange-looking symbols?"

"Kapu sticks," Roger replied quietly. "Taboo.

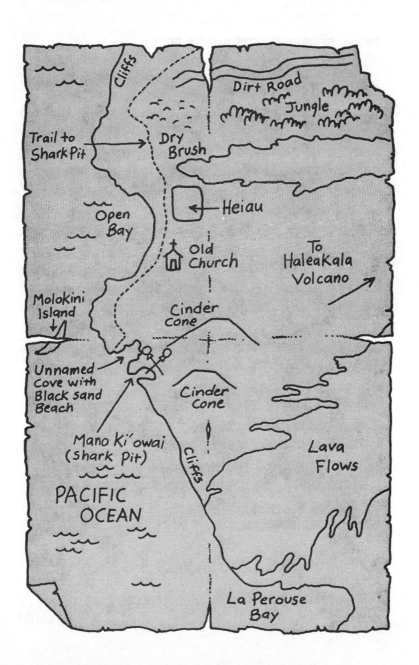

Forbidden. Keep out, Bruddah!"

"You mean—that's why the old Hawaiian was afraid to come here?"

"Kapu very strong in islands!" Roger replied, studying the map. "The old Hawaiians used to believe a person— like a kahuna* or priest—could pray a person to death."

"You're kidding!" Josh exclaimed.

Roger shook his head. "True! They believed. So a Hawaiian would stay away from a kapu area.

"Better for us," Roger continued. "Look at map, then look around us." He swung his free hand in a broad sweep. "Same landmarks! We're heading for the treasure!"

Josh and Tank studied the map, then looked around. Tank whispered, "Sure looks that way!"

Josh asked excitedly, "Are you saying the stranger is going to the same place marked on our map?"

"Looks like, Bruddah!"

Tank said, "Then that would mean the map the stranger stole and ours lead to the same thing!"

Josh frowned. "Dad said the editor told him it was some old historic artifact. We don't want anything like that! We want pirate's gold, or diver's black pearls or something like that!"

Roger refolded the map and put it in his pocket. "Hawaiian gold may be different, but still valuable."

Josh looked around, his blood speeding up again. "I don't see how the old Hawaiian you guys helped could have the same map that somebody else sent to the editor. I don't think it's the same!"

Tank agreed. "I don't either, but they're sure close together! Maybe we can look for ours while Mr. Ladd looks for his treasure!"

For a moment, Josh was tempted to tell Tank and Roger about deciding to follow Mr. Ladd when he went on alone. But before Josh could, his father called for the boys not to fall behind.

"Coming!" Josh called. He lowered his voice. "Well, whether there's one or two treasures down there, we can't let that stranger keep me from moving to these islands! We've got to find him!"

"Yeah!" Tank replied.

Roger asked softly, "How you going to stop him, Bruddahs?"

Josh didn't know, but he was determined to do whatever had to be done.

About fifteen minutes later, they arrived at a small, black sand beach complete with dense coconut trees. The kids dropped their snorkeling equipment while Mr. Ladd studied the ocean.

"Perfect!" he announced. "The reef's far out, so this area is shallow and protected. You can all snorkel close in, but don't wade in above your hips."

"Ah, Dad..."

Mr. Ladd interrupted. "Those are the rules! Also, stay together and don't swim alone! Now, I'm going to follow the coast. I don't expect any trouble, but if I'm not back by mid-afternoon, hike back to that little store and call the authorities."

Josh swallowed hard in sudden fear. "Dad, couldn't I go with—"

"Absolutely not, Son!" Mr. Ladd slung his flight bag back over his left shoulder and left the beach. He quickly passed through the palm trees and disappeared into the brush.

Roger whispered, "He's going same direction as our map!"

Tiffany called from the edge of the beach where she was walking barefooted on the strange black sand. "Hey, everybody, look at what I've found!"

Marsha warned, "Don't touch them! They're Portuguese men-of-war that've washed up on the beach."

"So?" Tiffany challenged.

The boys came closer to look. The sea creatures looked like pale-blue balloons. The transparent animals even had long string-like attachments.

Roger explained, "They sting! Hurt planty! Get infected sometimes."

Tank nodded. "Once I got one of their tentacles wrapped around my arm! I thought I was going to die from the pain!"

Josh wasn't interested. He had to follow his father before he was lost in the brush. However, maybe Josh didn't have to go alone. He motioned the boys to one side while the girls continued to explore the shoreline.

"We're so close," Josh began, "we should check out your map now! We may never get another chance."

Roger shook his head. "Your father said stay here."

"I know, but look at it this way: Dad may run into the stranger, and then he'd need our help."

Tank frowned. "I know, Josh, but you heard what he said: stay put."

Josh was determined. "Then I'll go alone."

His best friend sighed. "You know I can't let you do that. I'll go with you."

"Me know beddah," Roger said, "but me go, too."

The boys called to the girls that they were going exploring through the palms. That was fine with Tiffany and Marsha. They were going to put on fins and face masks with snorkels to go "eyeballing" (as they called it) in the shallow water.

Josh led Tank and Roger away from the beach. They tried to follow the way Mr. Ladd had gone, but promptly ran into dense stands of thorny kiawe. The lava underfoot was different from what they'd seen earlier. This had hardened in ripples that sliced their shoes like knives.

Josh stopped. "We've already lost him, and we can't get through here!"

Roger grinned. "You planty akamai*, Bruddah! Let's go back!"

Josh held up his hand. "Remember, if the stranger gets out of here with the artifact—whatever it is—then I can't move here to live! So why don't we go back to the beach, put on our gear and swim around to the place marked on the map?"

Roger shook his head vigorously. "No! Could get locked out!"

Josh asked, "What's that mean?"

Tank explained, "Oh, that's what happens when the waves break in a certain way. The surf and tide won't let a person get back to land."

"Could be carried out to sea," Roger added, pointing toward the horizon where ocean and sky seemed to meet.

Josh and Tank finally convinced the reluctant Roger to risk it for the treasure and to possibly help Mr. Ladd with the stranger. As the three boys started back toward the beach, there was a distant scream.

"That's Tiffany!" Josh cried. "Something's happened! Come on! Run!"

The three boys raced through the brush, heedless of the thorns. Josh was terrified of what was happening to his sister and her girlfriend. And it would be Josh's fault, because he'd disobeyed and left the girls alone.

Chapter Seven

THE SEA BECOMES AN ENEMY

Josh led Tank and Roger in a wild race through the coconut palms onto the black sand beach. Josh was fearful of what he'd see when he passed the last tree. He was somewhat relieved to see his sister and Marsha stumbling up out of the surf.

Then Josh realized Tiffany was doubled over. Her arms were crossed over her upper body. She sobbed with pain as Marsha supported her, but then she collapsed on her knees.

"What's the matter?" Josh called as he dashed breathlessly up to the girls.

Tiffany looked up with tears streaming down her wet face. "Oh, it hurts so bad!"

"What hurts?" Josh demanded. Then he saw the red welts starting to form on his sister's arms and rib cage.

It looked as though someone had taken a willow switch and hit her very hard, many times.

Marsha explained, "She got stung by a Portuguese man-of-war in the water!"

Josh was so relieved that the stranger hadn't hurt the girls that he took a deep breath and let it out very slowly.

"It hurrrts!" Tiffany moaned, still doubled over. "Can't we do something to stop it?"

Josh turned questioningly to Roger, the only one of the group who had been born in these islands.

Roger nodded. "Ammonia. Kind used to clean house."

Tank agreed. "That's right! Ordinary household ammonia! That's what they put on me when I got stung by one of those things!"

Josh looked at the whip-like welts still rising, red and angry-looking, on his suffering sister. He said, "They'd probably have some ammonia at that little store where we asked directions! I'll go get a bottle!"

"Wait!" Tiffany's voice was weak. "You'd have to go and come back! I can't stand the pain that long! I'll go myself and put the stuff on right away!"

"She's right," Marsha agreed. "That'll save half the time. I'll go with her. You guys stay here." And then Marsha and Tiffany hurried inland, leaving the boys alone on the beach.

Josh was sorry Tiffany had gotten stung, but he was greatly relieved that the stranger hadn't grabbed the girls. If anything terrible had happened, it would have been Josh's fault for disobeying his father.

Josh thought about his decision to follow his father today. Well, it was too late now to try going after him; at least by land. They'd never find Mr. Ladd in all that brush. Still, if Josh did nothing, and his father met the stranger alone. . .

Josh shivered as he thought of what that might mean. The stranger had Mr. Ladd's picture, so he'd recognize him. On the other hand, Mr. Ladd wouldn't know the stranger. That gave him the advantage, if they met. Even if the stranger wasn't dangerous, he might use force if he was cornered.

No matter what happened, if the stranger got away with the treasure—or whatever it was—there'd be no money for the Ladd family to move to Hawaii. That must not happen, Josh told himself fiercely. But what could he do now?

He looked out at the ocean and had an idea. "Hey, Roger, can I see that map again?"

Josh took the map and pointed out some things to Tank and Roger. He concluded, "There's absolutely no doubt our treasure site is right close! In fact, I wonder if it's not near where my father and the stranger are heading."

"Maybe so same t'ing," Roger said.

Josh rejected that idea. "If they are the same, that artifact stuff would be useless to us. But suppose there really are two separate places close together? Maybe one has old Hawaiian artifacts, and ours has pirates' treasure? Gold or jewels or something! Don't you see? We're so close! We've got to get to that place marked on the map and find out for sure what's there!"

Tank reminded Josh, "We've already tried overland, but

there's no way through that brush."

"My father got through," Josh reminded him. "Maybe the stranger did, too."

"We *think* your father got through," Tank replied. "Just because we couldn't find him doesn't mean he found the treasure or whatever it is."

"Sure t'ing, Bruddah!" Roger added. "He got no map; stranger does."

"We do have a map," Josh reminded them, tapping his forefinger on the paper. "And it shows this place is right on the oceanfront. So why can't we go there by water?"

Roger shook his head. We all pupule* do dat, Bruddah!"

Josh pushed his point. "It's not crazy! Look at the map again. See? We'll just swim out of this cove and around that point of land to the next cove."

Roger protested, "We don't know how far that is, or what it'll look like when we get there."

"Probably be a sandy beach like this!" Josh exclaimed.

"Maybe not, Bruddah!" Roger ran a brown finger along the map. "See those? Look like cliffs to me! Maybe no place to land!"

Josh tried to think how to convince Tank and Roger to change their minds. "Suppose that old Hawaiian's treasure is just waiting for us on the other side of this piece of land jutting out into the cove? And supposing the stranger beats my father to whatever it is they're after— then I couldn't live in Hawaii. Unless. . ."

He let his voice trail off, but Tank understood.

"Unless we find the old Hawaiian's treasure and it's enough so we can all be rich and you can move here to live!"

Josh smiled. "Finding that treasure would guarantee that!"

Tank hesitated. "You're not afraid of going into the water and maybe getting stung like your sister?"

"Marsha didn't get stung," Josh reminded the boys.

Tank still hesitated. "What would the girls think if they came back and we weren't here?"

"We'll leave them a note. I've got a pencil and paper. Come on, you guys! We're so close! Just around that point of land into the next cove!"

Tank and Roger exchanged glances, then shook their heads.

Josh shrugged. "Well, okay, then, but I'm not going to sit around and do nothing. I'm going 'eyeballing.' You want to come along?"

"Stay inside the reef?" Roger asked.

"Probably," Josh replied, looking at where the waves were breaking far out on the coral reef. "But we're all good swimmers, so what difference would that make?"

"Your father said to stay inside the reef," Tank reminded him.

"Okay," Josh agreed. "Let's see what it's like to look at fish eye-to-eye!"

All three boys sat down on the black sand beach and

removed their shoes. Each had come prepared. They pulled off their shirts and pants to reveal swim trunks underneath. They fitted face masks with snorkels on their foreheads. Roger and Tank also pulled fins over their feet. Josh left his fins on the sand and started wading into the blue-green water.

"Hey, Bruddah!"

Josh turned around to face Roger. "Yeah?"

"Moe bettah you malihini weah da kine* fins."

"Huh?" Josh asked.

Tank smiled and stood up with his fins in place. "He's telling you in Pidgin English that it's better for a newcomer like you to wear fins."

"Why?" Josh asked. "I'm a good swimmer, and this is about as safe a place as I've ever seen outside a swimming pool."

"Tide!" Roger said, standing and walking awkwardly into the water with his black fins. "Sometimes so strong, suck you out to sea!"

Josh turned to look over the bay. It was about as pretty and safe a spot as he could imagine. The water was so clear that he could see the dark horseshoe-shaped coral reef that kept big fish out of the sheltered, shallow water. The waves broke in beautiful white spray over the farthest part of the coral.

"I can handle this little place!" Josh said confidently. He turned to wade out into the bay.

"Pupule!" Roger called with a shake of his dark head

as he started into the water.

Josh protested. "I'm not crazy!"

Tank grinned. "I'm not so sure! Anyway, it wouldn't hurt you to wear fins." Tank pulled his mask down over his face and waded into the water. "One thing for sure: with that malihini skin, you'll sunburn fast! You're white as a fish's belly!" Tank slid onto his chest into the water and began swimming on the surface. His fins moved in a smooth motion that propelled his body forward without using his hands.

Josh took another look at the bay. "They're just trying to scare me," he muttered. He pulled his mask down over his face, put the snorkel's mouthpiece in place, lowered his face into the water and began to swim slowly on the surface.

Josh had never seen such fascinating numbers of small fish. And all of the fish were unlike anything he'd seen before off the coast of California. The face mask allowed him to see perfectly. The snorkel, sticking up above the water, permitted him to breathe normally. He swam easily, barely moving his arms so he wouldn't scare the fish. He used his feet in gentle kicking motions to keep him moving.

There were hundreds of fish of all colors, shapes and sizes; mostly quite small. "They're sure pretty!" he thought, "Wonder what kind they are?"

He moved on, enjoying the little fish. They didn't seem afraid of him, yet always kept just out of his reach. He forgot about the stranger and his father, fascinated by the new world he'd just discovered.

He came upon some coral that was so close to the surface he eased by, careful not to scratch his chest or legs on the sharp edges. There were dark holes in the coral. He remembered reading about moray eels that sometimes lived in such places. He knew the eels could give a swimmer a nasty bite. Josh was careful to keep his bare hands away from any place that might hide one of the big creatures.

As Josh moved past the coral, the swimming was easier. He barely even had to move his feet. He glided faster along the surface, but now the little fish were fewer, and the water seemed darker and not quite so clear.

Josh raised his head to check on the location of Tank and Roger. When Josh's face cleared the water, he found that he was no longer able to touch bottom. He automatically began treading water.

Tank and Roger were not in sight. The waves that had been breaking far out ahead of Josh were now behind him. For a second Josh frowned, trying to understand how that had happened.

He swiveled his head seaward. He was alone in that vast ocean.

"Whoops!" he exclaimed aloud, pulling his mask down again over his face and adjusting his mouthpiece. "Must've gone past the reef. Better get back closer to shore."

Josh began his usual smooth, strong, overhand strokes that had helped him win blue ribbons in swimming competition since he was a little kid. He kicked vigorously. But something was wrong. He felt as though he were going backward.

He again raised his head from the water, surprised to see how far away the black sand beach was. Josh glanced to both sides. The small cliffs of the bay that swung out from the beach seemed to be moving toward the shore. But cliffs didn't move!

Suddenly fearful, Josh kicked desperately and used his arms in fast, powerful strokes toward the beach. But it was useless.

The terrible truth hit Josh. "Without my fins, I'm being swept out to sea!"

Chapter Eight

A DARING PLAN GOES WRONG

"**O**h, Lord, no!" The surprised exclamation escaped the boy's lips. He tried harder, throwing all his strength into his arms and legs. But out of the corner of his eye he saw the cliffs still seeming to slide shoreward.

Since he had been a small boy, Josh had swum in the Pacific Ocean off Southern California's long coastline. He had always respected the power of the sea, but never had he felt so helpless!

Still, he didn't feel fear; only a sense of concern. "I can get out of this if I try hard enough," he told himself. Josh tried increasing the power and frequency of his arm and leg strokes. It was no use; he felt himself being sucked backward toward the vast, empty ocean.

He fought sudden panic and glanced around for any kind of way to help himself. There was nothing but the wide expanse of water. He breathed a silent, anguished prayer. "Help me, Lord. Please!"

There was no answer; nothing but the terrible sense of

sliding backward as though drawn by some immense power. He tried to keep calm, to think of a way out of his predicament. He felt his strength drain away as the powerful current carried him faster and faster out to sea.

"I'm going to drown!" he thought. "And it's my own fault!"

He had disobeyed his father's instructions to stay inside the reef. Josh remembered a verse his parents sometimes quoted. "Children, obey your parents in the Lord, for this is right. Honor your father and mother." There was something else about "so that you may have a long life."

Josh didn't want to think about that. He raised his head high out of the water to see better. Maybe Tank or Roger were nearby. Josh didn't want to call for help, exactly, but he would wave to them.

He scanned the water near the shore, but they were nowhere in sight.

Josh was caught in the unprotected sea where the waves rose high, then fell. He was carried up on a wave's crest, then plunged into a rolling trough that hid the beach and the cliffs. He still struggled, rolling his face from the water to take a breath and look to the left. He did that just as another wave hoisted him up high.

"I can't last much longer!" The thought hit him hard, just as a high wave lifted him momentarily.

For a second, he thought he saw Tank's concerned face, then the wave dumped Josh headfirst into the trough.

Something bumped his right shoulder. He swiveled his

head in panic, imagining a shark had bumped him. Josh had seen on the educational channel that sometimes sharks bumped a victim before striking. It was as though they were testing some strange creature before biting down with those fierce teeth.

"No! No!" Josh cried, swinging his right arm out in an automatic defensive gesture.

"Whassa mattah you, Bruddah?" Roger's startled voice seemed to be almost in Josh's right ear. "You still pupule?"

"Roger!" Josh sputtered, almost swallowing saltwater in his surprise.

"I'm going to grab your hand and tow you! Don't panic and grab me, or I'll have to let you go!"

Wordlessly, Josh nodded. An enormous sigh of relief escaped his lips as Roger's strong hand closed over Josh's right wrist. He saw the local boy roll over on his side, kick powerfully with his fins and stroke with his free hand.

Josh felt himself stop moving seaward. He kicked with his feet and stroked with his left hand. Roger gave him a hard jerk, sending Josh skimming slightly ahead. Roger let go of his hand, and Josh had a momentary sense of panic. Was Roger deserting him?

Josh saw Tank just ahead. He swung around, grabbed Josh by the wrist and rolled over. At the same instant, Josh felt Roger reach under his armpit and give him a shove toward shore.

Tank yelled. "Swim like you've never done before!"

Josh stifled a half-sob and obeyed.

It seemed to take forever to get inside the reef. But propelled by the fins, the three boys together made headway...until an incoming wave caught the boys and rolled them gently to the beach. All three lay there at the water's edge, breathing hard, too spent to stand.

"Tank, Roger...thanks," he said softly when he regained his breath.

Roger scowled at him. "You almost got us all drowned!"

"I know. I'm...sorry."

Tank muttered, "Next time, wear your fins!"

Josh nodded, too weary and ashamed to say more.

When he felt stronger, Josh looked inland. There was no sign of his sister or Marsha. Well, they'd be back soon, he was sure, and Tiffany's stings wouldn't be hurting anymore.

Josh let his eyes sweep off to the direction his father had gone. Was he safe? Had he met the stranger? Did the stranger beat him to the artifact? Was the family going to have to give up the idea of moving to Hawaii?

The questions bothered Josh tremendously. He got up, pulled on his shirt to keep from getting sunburned, and began idly exploring the beach. Tank and Roger were stretched out on the black sand, enjoying the sun.

Josh came to a downed palm tree. The trunk and roots rested on the shore with the palm fronds in the water.

Josh sank upon the tree trunk and gazed out toward the reef. There the surf rose in silent white spray as it hit the underwater coral. It seemed impossible that he had been so far out! His eyes lifted slightly toward the horizon. He had come close to being carried helplessly out where the vast sky and ocean seemed to meet, never again to feel the shore.

The boy's head dropped and his eyes closed in painful memory. When he opened them again, the sunlight reflected from something under the log near the fronds. Josh leaned forward to see better.

"Hey!" His startled cry brought Tank and Roger running.

"Wraparound sunglasses!" Josh held them up for the others to see. "Just like the stranger wore!"

Tank shrugged. "That doesn't prove he was here. Lots of people wear those kinds of shades!"

Josh knelt by the log and scraped away a suspicious pile of sand. He uncovered a small plastic bag and held it up.

"No, but this does! A man's clothes! And look! That's a picture of my dad! The stranger *has* been here! Maybe he didn't beat my dad to the place!"

The excited boys closely examined the sand. Roger pointed. "Scuba tank made that mark! Rubber boat made those! See?"

The boys bent to look more closely. Josh and Tank exchanged glances and nodded. A small inflatable boat and scuba diving gear had been here, but now they were gone.

Josh forgot his recent near-drowning experience in the excitement of the discovery. "The stranger must have rowed out of this bay to approach the land again! But which way? Right or left?"

"That way!" Tank exclaimed, pointing toward the direction Mr. Ladd had gone.

"Wait!" Roger cried. He ran to where his pants were rolled up on a small rattan mat. He dug into the pockets and hurried back, unfolding his map.

The boys gathered around and discussed the situation. They stared in thoughtful contemplation to the left. They looked at each other and nodded.

Josh spoke decisively. "That's got to be it! Only my Dad went overland and the stranger went by water! My Dad's probably in danger right now! No matter whether he or the stranger got there first, the other'll have time to get there! They'll run into each other, and the stranger has the advantage in size and recognizing Dad! I've got to help him!"

"How?" Tank asked. "We tried to get through those thorns and couldn't!"

"And," Roger added, "We almost lost you to the sea!"

Josh took a few quick steps in the black sand while his mind raced. Then he stopped and faced his friends.

"I've got to swim out and try to find him before it's too late!"

"Pupule again!" Roger exploded, slapping his open

right palm against his forehead. "You forget so soon what almost happened to you out there?"

"I won't go out so far!" Josh announced. "I'll wear fins and stay in close to the shore! I'll follow those cliffs around that point of land! There must be another bay just on the other side!"

Tank studied the situation and nodded. "That might work! The waves aren't very big against those cliffs."

Josh asked, "Roger, do you think I'd get caught in the tide and sucked out if I stayed close to those cliffs?"

He shook his head. "No, that's probably okay. But the danger could be on the other side."

"Why is that?" Josh asked.

"Like I said before," Roger replied, "you could get locked out. The waves sometimes form so that they won't let a person back in to shore."

Josh thought fast. His father almost surely was in danger from the stranger, who could slip up on Mr. Ladd from the ocean side. Josh glanced again at the water. It was fairly calm some distance off the cliffs of the bay.

"I'm a good swimmer, especially with fins and face mask! I can work my way along the shore around the corner to where there's a place to land."

Roger was doubtful. "There may be nothing but lava cliffs on the other side, with no place to go ashore." He consulted the map. "See? This beach where we are is marked, but there's nothing on the other side except that little cove with those Hawaiian words on it."

Josh said, "I saw those earlier and wondered what they meant. Roger, you understand Hawaiian; what do they mean?"

He shrugged. "Like everybody else, I speak some Hawaiian and know many words. But I don't know these two: 'Mano* Ki'owai*.'"

"Mahn-oh," Josh repeated. "Hmm? I think maybe that's Spanish. Means 'hand,' I think. But Kee-oh-why-ee—that's definitely Hawaiian. Tank, you got any clue as to what it means?"

"Well, since it's written right over the water in the cove, maybe it means water or something."

Josh raised his eyes to look at the spit of land that separated their beach from whatever was indicated on the map before them. He shrugged and glanced back at the map.

His finger moved farther inland on the map. "Well, we know what heiau means, because that was explained when we came to it. That was the temple grounds. And hale pule* means church; I know that much. We saw the ruins of that earlier. So we've seen everything marked on the map except this mano ki'owai and the place with the kapu sticks."

Tank said, "The kapu marks must be what your father and the stranger are trying to reach."

"But Dad went by land and the stranger by sea, here and here," he said, touching the map in two close-by places. Josh looked again at the point of land and tried to envision what it was really like on the other side of the left cliff. "Anyway, there'll be someplace to land because the stranger had a map and he went by water. So I'm going to try it."

He returned to where he'd left the rented equipment, and pulled off his shirt. He then donned the mask with snorkel, followed by the fins.

His friends watched him in silence.

Josh said, "I've got to try helping my dad!"

Tank and Roger didn't answer.

Josh stood up and began awkwardly moving toward the water with the fins on his feet. "Don't you want me to try helping him so I can move to Hawaii?"

Both boys nodded.

Josh continued, "Then I've got to do it!"

As he waded into the surf, Tank called. "Wait! I'll go with you!"

Roger shrugged. "Now I'm pupule," he said, "but— okay."

The boys left a note for the girls, donned their fins and face masks with snorkels. Josh led the way into the water, trying not to think about what had happened to him just a short time before.

The other boys followed Josh past the left end of the protective reef. His concern grew as he swam strongly, using his fins to stay close to the cliffs. He kept half-expecting the terrible tug at his body as before, but the tide did not suck at him this time. Due to the fins, he was able to maintain a sense of control. He glanced back. Tank and Roger were close behind. Josh turned to watch where he was going.

They came to land's end without trouble and swam abreast around the point. A small, pretty cove opened before them. Josh let out a joyful yell. "It's perfect! Come on! Let's get to shore!"

Tank asked, "Where are you going to land? There's no beach! Just cliffs!"

For the first time, Josh saw the shore. There were only strange-looking black cliffs unlike any he had ever seen. They weren't tall; perhaps no more than twenty or thirty feet. But the cliffs rose straight up out of the sea. The black mass swept off in both directions like a great wall.

Josh didn't like the looks of that at all. He swam forward, trying for a better look. Suddenly, something invisible but powerful seemed to move against his chest. He frowned, trying to swim against the strange, unseen force, but his forward progress was stopped. He turned to look questioningly at Tank and Roger.

The island boy took a couple of quick strokes sideways. His dark eyes were wide. He whispered, "Feel that? We're locked out!"

Chapter Nine

THE SEA'S TERRIBLE SECRET

"**L**ocked out?" Josh repeated, treading water and raising the mask from his face to his forehead. "You mean we can't get any closer?" He motioned toward the black, foreboding cliffs.

Roger nodded and pushed his mask up. The snorkel bobbed like a giant insect's antenna. "Can't go forward."

Tank joined the two other boys in treading water. "What'll we do?"

"Swim out sideways," Roger replied. He jerked his head to his left, indicating the near point of land around which they'd just swum. "Go around."

"Can we do it?" Josh asked anxiously.

"Got to try, Bruddah!" Roger pulled his mask down over his face and adjusted his snorkel mouthpiece.

The other boys did the same, and then swam together toward the near point of land they had just passed. Josh sensed at once that they were not making any progress. The invisible barrier was not only ahead of them, it also circled to their left.

Roger stopped swimming. "No good that way! Still locked out! Try to the right!"

Josh swallowed hard, nodded, but didn't speak. All three boys turned and struck out toward the far shore.

It wasn't a very big cove to cross, Josh thought with a surge of hope. Even here at the end where the last bit of land gave way to the open sea, the cove entrance wasn't wider than the length of a football field.

The color of the water was different here from what it had been near the black sand beach. The cove's water was an intense blue, yet clear enough that he could see the white sand bottom. It didn't seem more than ten feet below Josh's face mask.

He swam strongly, trying to avoid thinking about what a terrible spot they might be in if they were still locked out to the right. He kicked hard to pull up even with Roger.

"If we're still locked out over there, how far around do we have to swim?"

"Don't know! Sometimes miles!"

Josh almost groaned. What kind of a mess had he gotten them into?

The three boys swam in silence until they were within thirty feet or so of the far cove wall. Josh saw Roger turn toward the black lava cliffs and tentatively try swimming toward them. He let out a yell.

"No more lockout! Be okay now!"

Josh joyfully kicked toward the cliffs. He saw waves

breaking against the sheer face of the cliffs. He started to call out that he didn't see a place to land when Tank swam alongside.

"Hey, I'm tired! Let's lay on our backs awhile and rest. Okay?"

"Okay," Josh replied. "But while we float, let's look for a place to land."

All three boys rolled over onto their backs and kicked gently with their fins to keep themselves on the surface and parallel to the frowning cliffs.

Josh studied them. From the map given his father by the car rental company, Josh knew the cliffs had been formed centuries ago when Haleakala erupted. The molten lava had flowed into the sea, forming cliffs that were now hardened like stone. The black cliffs had some spots that were a reddish-brown color. Green plants about eight inches tall grew near the cliff tops where small amounts of soil had formed over the years.

"You know what?" Josh asked. "This place looks kind of familiar. I think I've been here before—but that's not possible."

Roger snorted. "No see dis kine place befoah, Bruddah!"

Josh smiled. "I keep meaning to ask you, Roger: how come you can speak English perfectly, yet sometimes you talk funny like just now?"

"Practice, Bruddah!" Roger answered with a grin. "Don't want to talk like da kine malihini all time! Some kids at school t'ink I act too smaht; maybe so smack me alongside head!"

Tank raised his head from the water. "Hey! There's a place to land!" He pointed. "See? Right at the base of that funny-looking part that has the big crack in it! Just this side of that crack is a kind of shelf!"

Roger said, "Yes! Just above the high-water line! Big enough for us!"

Josh saw it then. "You're right! After we land, we'll find a way to climb that cliff above it and get on top. That's where my father must have gone!"

He hurriedly adjusted his mouthpiece and pulled the mask down over his face. "Let's go!"

Roger and Tank started swimming fast toward the lava shelf. Josh fell behind, delayed by some strange sense of fear or dread. He studied the cliffs above the landing site. "That's where Dad must have gone. Wonder if he's in danger from the stranger?"

Josh realized saltwater was seeping into his mouth because he had improperly adjusted his snorkel. He stopped swimming and treaded water to refit his mouthpiece. He dropped it.

"Ahh!" he muttered in disgust, watching the mouthpiece sinking toward the white sand bottom.

"Hey!" he called to the boys swimming a few feet ahead of him, "I dropped my mouthpiece! You go ahead and I'll catch up with you in a minute!"

Tank swiveled his head and called, "Okay!" And then

both boys swam on toward the landing site.

Josh started to pulled his mask down over his face again so he could see more clearly under water. As he did, he was struck again by the strange feeling that he'd been here before. Shrugging off the idea, he made a surface dive to retrieve the mouthpiece.

The water was so clear and blue that Josh could still see the mouthpiece dropping toward the bottom. He did a quick tuck, stuck his feet straight up and kicked the fins hard, driving himself down rapidly. The mouthpiece continued to sink slowly ahead of him. Josh kicked harder and used his forearms to catch up, but he didn't seem to be gaining.

The pressure on his ears warned him that he was diving deeper and deeper. He knew he was already farther down than any swimming pool in which he'd ever dived. Still, the bottom seemed to be about the same distance away.

"The depth's deceiving," he thought, feeling his lungs begin to complain about holding the same breath so long. "It could be a hundred feet to the bottom! I don't need that mouthpiece enough to chase it any deeper!"

He reversed his direction and kicked his fins to drive him upward. It was surprising how far away the surface seemed. By the time he could see the sun's brightness in the water and knew the surface was just ahead, his lungs ached for air. He used his hands to stroke upward faster.

Out of the corner of his eye, he saw a sudden movement.

He swung his head that way. A shadow moved there; a long, slender shadow that blended and vanished into the sea.

"Shark!"

Josh's mind exploded with the thought. His heart thumped with sudden fright, then he scolded himself. "Nah! Couldn't be!" He kept swimming steadily upward while half-fearfully watching the area where he'd seen the movement. He saw nothing.

He broke the surface and gulped air. He wanted to call out to Tank and Roger, but told himself, "No sense scaring them! Probably was just my imagination!"

But supposing it *had* been a shark? Josh's inclination was to splash wildly toward shore, but he forced himself to swim evenly, avoiding any sign of panic. He remembered from educational television programs that sharks seemed more likely to attack anything in the water that behaved strangely, as a wounded fish might.

"Was it a shark or wasn't it?" Josh asked himself as he rapidly neared the safety of the tiny, rough lava shelf that jutted out at the base of the strange cliffs.

Without the mouthpiece for his snorkel, he had to hold his breath and stick his face underwater. He swung his face mask back and forth, quickly checking everything in the near vicinity. There was nothing; no shadow, no movement; not even small fish.

"Guess I imagined it," he told himself. His fear eased. He continued swimming toward the shore, his face underwater. A strange and fascinating world floated by.

There was no kelp as off California's shores. He could see coral here, closer to the cliffs. Some of it was shaped like a human brain. The white sand bottom was much nearer than when he'd dropped his mouthpiece. Now lots of tiny, brightly colored tropical fish darted about. The water seemed to almost have a rainbow in it because of the filtered sunshine.

It was peaceful and quiet under the surface. Josh relaxed, knowing the lava shelf was close by. He swam closer to the black cliffs, noticing that they changed underwater. Some looked like dark openings to caves or tubes.

The openings on these strange lava formations ranged from as little as a foot around to maybe six to ten feet. They were dark, so that Josh couldn't see back inside, giving them a scary look. One even reminded Josh of the entrance to an abandoned mine shaft his father had once shown him in California's Gold Rush country.

Thinking of his father made Josh raise his face from the water. He took a breath and glanced ahead to see how close he was to the landing shelf. Just a few more strokes.

He glanced up to the top of the cliffs. Suddenly, his heart leaped wildly and he swallowed hard.

"Those two funny-shaped things on top of the cliffs!" he muttered, looking hard at them through his mask. They somewhat resembled pyramids, except their tops were worn off. One was perhaps four hundred feet high; the other about half that.

Josh thought with panic, "They must be cinder cones*! And what did I just see underwater? Lava tubes?"

He glanced fearfully around, his mind racing with a terrible realization. "Now I know why this place looks familiar! This is what I saw in the color photographs which Dad and the stranger had!"

Josh started to shout his discovery to his two friends swimming ahead. Roger was just raising his face from the water. He turned and jerked off his mask. His dark eyes were wide with fright.

"Sharks!" Roger yelled. "Those big lava tubes are filled with sharks!"

Too late, Josh realized they had blundered into the Shark Pit!

Chapter Ten

TRAPPED IN THE SHARK PIT

"Don't kid about things like that!" Tank snapped. Roger pointed to the water below the cliffs. "See for yourself! I'm getting out of here!"

Josh and Tank immediately stuck their face masks under the water. Josh was already afraid he'd seen a shark; now he was fearful he'd see more. Yet he had to be sure.

The clear blue water allowed total visibility for some distance, beyond which a pale blue wall seemed to start. At first, Josh didn't see anything moving. Even the little fish had vanished. Taking deep breaths, the two boys tucked and made a shallow surface dive. They swam cautiously toward the underwater lava tubes. Their dark openings slowly appeared ahead.

Suddenly, Josh backpeddled hard with hands and legs, bringing himself to a full stop. He reached out and grabbed Tank's left shoulder. Josh started to point, but it wasn't necessary. Tank had seen, too!

The tubes lay like irregular-sized concrete pipes at a construction site on land. A few moments before, Josh hadn't been able to see anything except dark holes.

Now every tube opening seemed to be patrolled by at least one shark! They ranged from about three feet long to twice Josh's length.

He spun toward Tank, whose eyes were wide with fright behind the mask.

Josh raised both hands, palms outward, in a calming motion. He jerked his head upward and slowly brought his legs into play. The fins propelled him upward. Tank was right beside him.

They broke the surface together. Immediately Josh warned, "Don't panic! Don't splash! Just swim for the shelf—easy! easy!"

"They'll get us!" Tank cried, striking out overhand for the only possible landing site.

"Maybe not if we don't make them think we're hurt!" Josh forced himself to take steady strokes and kick his fins evenly. "I've seen lots of shark programs on television! They probably won't bother us if we don't act panicky!"

He glanced around for Roger but didn't see him. For a horrible moment, he thought maybe the sharks had already attacked him.

Josh turned to look at the shelf, hoping to see Roger there. The shelf glistened wetly, black and empty of life. Josh kept swimming rapidly but steadily, seeing Tank's frightened face even with his own.

Josh tried to calm his racing heart by remembering how

many television programs he'd seen where divers swam among dozens of sharks. Sometimes the divers had fed the sharks, setting off a feeding frenzy; yet the swimmers hadn't been hurt.

Something bumped Josh's side. In sudden terror, he twisted and looked down. A shark at least twelve feet long veered away, his rough hide scraping against the boy's bare rib cage.

Josh instinctively kicked out. He felt the fin connect with the great beast. The shark gave a rapid flip of the tail and vanished into the pale blue wall.

At the same time, Josh saw a shark's fin break the surface twenty feet away. This was immediately followed by another and another! They moved slowly toward the boys.

Tank had seen the sharks, too. He tried to say something, but nothing came out. His mouth worked soundlessly, but he managed to point under the water.

A long, dark shape showed a few feet under the surface. Josh took a quick breath and lowered his face into the water. His heart seemed to stop!

The great shark's round black eyes seemed fixed on Josh's legs, slowly treading water with the fins. The shark moved effortlessly, closer and closer to the boy.

He seemed frozen in place, too frightened to swim; paralyzed by the sight of the terrible monster easing toward him. Josh couldn't take his eyes off the huge predator.

It moved unhurriedly, its long body and tail propelling

him ever-closer to the defenseless boy.

Josh felt shivers shake his whole body. Even though the water was warm, Josh felt his flesh crawling with goose bumps.

"What've I done?" he thought wildly. "If I'd only listened to what Dad told me to do!"

Josh's need for air forced him to raise his head from the water. He tried to do that without panic. He only had time to gulp once, but in that moment he felt the sunshine on his face.

A quick glance showed more shark fins on the surface and the safe lava shelf close by. A few quick strokes would take him to safety. He could see Tank was almost to the shelf. But the horrible fear that the sharks would strike from below made Josh stick his face back in the water to be sure how close the nearest shark was.

It was perhaps fifteen feet away. The unblinking, seemingly dead black eyes were locked on the helpless boy. Several other sharks drifted silently out of the deep blue shadows into clear visibility. They stood out sharply against the white sand bottom. All moved toward the boy, now alone in the water.

Josh made up his mind. It was a desperate gamble to hurry, but it was too terrifying to stay still while the great creatures closed in on him.

He kicked hard with the fins, driving him into full motion. At the same instant, he twisted in the air and struck out furiously, swimming frantically toward the safety of the shelf.

He dared not allow himself to look back or down into the water. He reached out wildly with his right hand, stroking mightily on the surface.

Something seized his hand and clamped down hard!

He was so startled he jerked back and yelled in terror, "No! No!"

He started to strike out with his free hand just as his wild eyes recognized Roger. He was crouched on the shelf, hanging onto Josh's right wrist with both hands. Tank was beside him, reaching out to Josh.

"We've got you!" Tank called, grabbing Josh's other wrist. "Come on, Roger! Pull!"

Their combined efforts yanked Josh bodily from the water and onto the rough shelf. The coral sliced and scratched his chest and chin, but Josh didn't care.

He was safe! He lay flat on his stomach, gasping for breath, too weak from fear to speak or move. His legs with the black fins on his feet still extended over the water.

Suddenly, Josh heard water explode behind him. He glanced back just as a great long snout shot up from the water. The jaws opened wide, showing fearsome teeth. The protective opaque shield slid shut over the big round eye. The horrifying mouth snapped shut on Josh's right foot.

Josh shrieked and automatically rolled over on his side, kicking with his left foot and trying to pull his right foot free. The shark shook it violently back and forth. Josh saw his black fin flop crazily in the air, and then slide free.

Instantly, the shark dived. Josh felt Tank and Roger seize him under the shoulders and pull back hard.

Fearfully, Josh glanced down. His fin was gone, but the foot was still there!

Josh collapsed with a shudder on the rough lava shelf.

It took a long time for the three boys to calm down. When Josh could stand on weak, trembling legs, he wordlessly hugged both Tank and Roger. Josh realized they had twice saved his life today, and both times he had gotten into trouble through his own foolishness.

He was ashamed, but he didn't know how to say that, so he suggested, "Let's see how we can get off of this shelf."

Still trembling, Josh walked unsteadily toward the black cliffs. He gingerly picked his way across the rough lava which hurt his bare feet. The shelf was about thirty feet long and twenty feet wide.

It had apparently been made centuries ago when some of the molten lava pouring into the sea had cooled and formed a nearly level area. Subconsciously, Josh was aware of the sticky feeling on his skin from the saltwater drying. He smelled the familiar pineapple juice fragrance common to Hawaiian waters.

"Hey!" he exclaimed, "What's that?"

A moment later he bent down to examine the object that had caught his eye. He raised his voice to call, "Hey, you guys! Here's the rubber boat—or what's left of it!"

The boys hurried to examine the one-man craft. It lay punctured on the hard lava on the far side of the rough shelf.

Josh nodded. "Well, we know the stranger got here, but where'd he go with that scuba gear? Come on, let's look some more."

The boys went back to the cliffs. They rose steep and straight. In times past, the magma, or molten material which had formed beneath the earth's crust, had flowed down from the erupting volcano toward the sea.

The molten rock had been something like a chocolate frosting on a cake. The lava had long since hardened on the surface of the original cliff. Under the water, some of the lava had curled over and solidified into tubes.

Josh shaded his eyes against the sun. "It'd slice our hands and feet to ribbons if we tried to climb that cliff," he said. "Not to mention our bare chests and legs."

Tank said slowly, "Well, it's a cinch we're not going back into that water with those sharks!"

Roger agreed with a shudder. "We're alive but with no way out!"

Josh swallowed hard, realizing it was his fault. He didn't want to dwell on that thought because he already felt terribly guilty. He tried to sound cheerful.

"The girls may be back from the store by now! They'll find our note and get help!"

Tank nodded slowly. "Seems like our only chance."

A terrible thought hit Josh. Even if that happened, it

might be too late to help his father. Right at this moment, Mr. Ladd could be facing the mysterious stranger close by. But where? He forced himself to sound cheerful.

"The stranger got off of this shelf, and so can we! Keep looking!"

Josh again examined the cliffs for the most logical way off. There was a break between the shelf and the cliffs. A kind of narrow trough or channel had been formed there. Seawater surged noisily through it. Both ends were partially blocked by chunks of lava that let the sea ebb and flow, but prevented sharks from entering.

"Nothing here." He turned his head to look at the dark shadows moving in the water around the shelf.

Tank and Roger joined him. Tank pointed to the sharks. "Maybe they got him."

Josh shook his head. "I don't think so. The stranger came prepared with scuba gear and the map, so he must have known exactly where he was going. Too bad we don't have our map."

Tank's slow voice sounded gloomy. "Well, we don't! We don't have anything except our swim trunks and gear. No food, no water, nothing! Besides, Roger and I have pretty good suntans, but you've got that malahini white skin! You'll get a terrible sunburn if we stay out here much longer!"

Josh glanced down at his body. He was definitely showing pink that could turn quite painful if he stayed out in the rays much longer. But how could he get off this shelf?

He swept his hands in front of the cliffs. "The secret to where the stranger went has to be right here; right before our eyes, somewhere!"

"Maybe so, but we don't see it!" Tank drawled.

As the water surged out into the cove again, Josh saw something. "Hey, look here!" he called, leaning forward.

When Tank and Roger were also bent over looking closely, Josh pointed. "See it? Something's been carved right into the lava! A drawing!"

"I see it!" Roger whispered. "Kapu sign!"

Tank mused, "Keep out! But what could be forbidden about that cliff? There's nothing except lava!"

"No, look!" Josh jabbed a finger at the mark. "There's something else just below the kapu sign! See? Looks like the top of a tunnel or cave!"

"An underwater cave!" Tank whispered. "It could be!"

"Sure t'ing, Bruddah!" Roger cried. "Lots of caves in Hawaii."

"But an underwater one!" Josh said softly. "A grotto, I think it's called! I've read that Hawaii has some of these, too!" He stood up triumphantly. "That's where the stranger must have gone with his scuba gear! Tank, let me borrow your snorkeling gear and flippers!"

"What're you going to do?" Tank asked with alarm in his voice.

"I got you guys into this mess, so I've got to get you out. Besides, I've got to try helping my Dad."

Tank exclaimed in disbelief, "You're not going in that

cave!"

"Got to try!" Josh answered. "The stranger went somewhere, and that's the only logical place!" Josh picked up his friend's gear, pulled on the fins and adjusted the snorkel and face mask.

Tank asked, "What if you run into him?"

"Don't know yet." Josh said. "But he can't be any more danger to us than what we've got here. Besides, I've got to try to help my Dad."

Against Tank and Roger's protests, Josh eased into the trough. He stood tensely before what little portion he could see of the cave's opening. He took a deep breath and submerged.

Trying to control his fear, Josh extended his hands before him and kicked with his fins. He was instantly propelled into the total silence and darkness of a grave.

His probing hands felt solid walls on both sides. "It's too narrow to turn around!" he thought with sudden terror. "Can I back out if I have to?"

He swam on through the still blackness, knowing the air he held in his lungs might be all that was between him and a terrible end.

He felt the tug of the water against his body and realized the water in the trough was going out. A moment later, it changed as the water rushed back in.

Suddenly, he felt the ball in the end of his snorkel pop loose. His thoughts exploded into terror.

"Oh, no! My snorkel's failed!"

Chapter Eleven

THE STRANGER STRIKES

Josh instantly held his breath so he wouldn't get water in his nostrils. The ball at the end of the borrowed snorkel was made to close automatically when the diver submerged. When the ball was above water, it released itself so the swimmer could breathe while keeping his face in the water. Since Josh had just felt the ball release, either it had failed, or else it was above water.

Cautiously, while his heart beat so fast he could hear it against his ears, he tested what had happened. He took a tiny breath. He didn't inhale water. "Air!"

He surfaced carefully. Through his face mask, he made out a nearly dark tunnel with a low ceiling. Then he realized he had come up inside an underground chamber.

"It is a grotto!" he thought. "And I'm breathing fresh air! But how does it get here? Not from the shelf, so it's got to come from—there."

He faced away from the ocean, back into the unknown darkness of the grotto. Some kind of light seemed to be reflecting on the water farther back.

Suddenly hopeful, Josh started surface-swimming toward the light, then stopped. Had he heard voices? Men's voices?

Josh brought his legs into position to tread water so he could listen better, but his feet touched bottom. Carefully, unable to believe it, he tested again. Shallow! He was standing in hip-deep water.

He didn't hear the voices anymore. Or had he heard them at all? Perhaps it was only his imagination. Being as silent as possible, he waded toward the light. It seemed to come from around a curve in the grotto.

Josh ran his fingers lightly along the cool walls and low ceiling so he wouldn't bang his head on something in the gloom. He didn't hear the voices anymore. "Maybe I imagined them," he told himself.

As he followed the grotto around the slight curve, Josh stopped in surprise. The grotto opened into a large, dry cave. It was about thirty feet high and at least as wide. The grotto water and the gently sloping cave floor met a couple of yards ahead of Josh.

A shaft of sunlight poured through an opening in the cave's roof. Josh saw that it was a Hawaiian burial chamber with wooden spears, a giant surfboard, bone fish hooks and other artifacts. A complete skeleton of a large person was barely visible in the shadows. A length of red nylon rope trailed from the cave's opening down to the floor.

"Dad's rope!" Josh thought. "He must have lowered

himself that way! But—where is he?"

Josh strained to see better in the uncertain light before calling out. He caught a movement and made out Mr. Ladd. He was sitting down on the cave floor, his back to the wall. A big man in a glistening black wet suit was bending over him.

"Well, now, mister!" the man said with satisfaction. "I guess that piece of rope will hold you while I clean out this place!"

Josh recognized the stranger's voice.

Mr. Ladd said, "You've got no right—"

"Shut up!" the stranger interrupted, straightening up. "Otherwise, when I'm safely back on the Mainland, I might forget to tell somebody where you are—before it's too late!"

Josh unthinkingly made a sound in the water. The stranger spun around and saw the boy. With a startled exclamation, the man plunged into the water after Josh.

He whirled and dived head first into the grotto's shallow waters. The stranger was faster.

Josh felt a big hand grab his right ankle just above the fin. The boy struggled to free himself, but strong arms jerked him out of the water.

"Hold still, kid! Where'd you come from?"

Josh struggled to free himself. "Let me go! Tank! Roger!" The works mocked him as they echoed off into the grotto and cave.

"I said, hold still!" the stranger growled through

clenched teeth. He lifted Josh so hard his head smashed into the grotto's low ceiling.

Josh's brain seemed to explode with brilliant white light. Then a darkness settled down fast and Josh slumped unconscious in the stranger's arms.

Just how much time passed, Josh had no idea. But the next thing the boy knew, he seemed to be hearing his father's voice from a long way off. Josh tried to answer, but couldn't. His head hurt and it was awfully dark, although his eyes were open.

"Josh! Wake up!" Mr. Ladd's voice was closer for a moment, then it faded. "Untie me so I can look after my son!"

Josh tried to say, "I'm okay, Dad," but no words came. He could make out his father sitting beside him. Josh heard another voice and knew it was the stranger's.

"Look, mister, I'm sorry about your kid! But it was an accident, like I said!"

Josh heard his father speak again, low and hard. There was something in it Josh had never heard before.

"If anything happens to my son, I'll see that you're brought to justice if it takes the rest of my life!"

"Relax, mister! I'm no killer! Sure, I burglarized you a few times until I got the map, but I didn't hurt you a while ago, and I didn't mean to hurt your boy! Now quit bothering me while I gather this stuff up and get out of here!"

Mr. Ladd said firmly, "Those artifacts belong to the

people of Hawaii!"

The stranger chuckled. "You were going to take them for yourself, but I beat you to them!"

"No, I was going to write a magazine article about the discovery and turn the rest over to the state! Please! Untie me so I can help my son!"

Josh's head was clearing fast. He looked around and blinked hard. Within a few minutes the boy remembered everything and knew he was lying on the cool damp floor of the cave. By the filtered light from the hole overhead, Josh saw his father's hands were bound behind his back with a piece of red rope. It had apparently been cut from the long one hanging from the hole in the roof.

An idea popped into Josh's head. He carefully moved his hand toward his father's leg. Instead, Josh felt the stranger's air tank where he'd set it down. Josh's hand moved on until he gently touched his father's leg.

Josh heard his father suck in a short, surprised breath. He leaned forward over his son and started to speak.

Josh stopped him. He whispered, "Shh! Don't say anything! Let me try to untie your hands."

He heard his father give a long, low sigh of relief and mutter, "Thank God!"

The stranger was over against the far wall of the cave. He was playing a flashlight beam around.

"What'd you say?" he asked, turning around.

"I...I was just saying a little prayer."

The man grunted and went on with his examination.

Josh forgot his aching head. He tried to not think about how all of the terrible things that had happened were his fault. If he hadn't disobeyed his father...

Josh tried to console himself by saying he had really been trying to help his dad, but he knew that didn't make up for his disobedience.

Josh kept working on the knots, but his mind jumped about. He thought of Tank and Roger, stuck on that lava shelf with the sharks around them. They were probably worried sick about what had happened to him.

And what about Tiffany and Marsha? Had they returned from the little store and found the note?

Josh forced the fearful thoughts from his mind and concentrated on the knot. It was loosening slightly. But even when it was free, what could one man and a boy do against the powerful stranger?

The man's flashlight flickered in Josh's direction. He froze, eyes closed, until the light moved on.

The stranger said, "I'm going to tie a load of this junk onto that rope and pull it out of the hole at the top. But maybe I'd better check your hands first."

Josh felt his father stiffen. At first, Josh thought it was because of the stranger's remark. But Mr. Ladd wasn't looking at the stranger as he approached with the flashlight.

Josh followed his father's eyes. Mr. Ladd snapped his head around quickly to look at the stranger, but Josh stared into the grotto.

Had he heard a noise?

The stranger dropped something he was carrying. With a curse, he bent to retrieve it.

Mr. Ladd whispered fiercely, "How close are you, Son?"

He whispered back. "Almost got it! Another few seconds...."

"Uh-oh! Here he comes again!"

Josh felt his heart sink! He was so close and yet so far from freeing his father. Josh desperately glanced around for something to use in self-defense. He saw his father's flight bag, now sagging empty next to him. Or was it?

"Dad's camera!" Josh thought. He plunged his hand into the open bag and grabbed the straps. He leaped up, pulling the heavy camera free. He thought of swinging it like the shepherd boy David had whirled a sling at Goliath. But could Josh connect with the stranger who had stopped in surprise?

Josh stood, legs spread and braced, before his defenseless father. Josh warned the stranger, "Don't come any closer!"

The stranger snapped the flashlight's beam into the boy's eyes. Josh automatically turned away from the light, but bright spots with black circles danced and flickered before him.

Even though temporarily blinded, Josh tried to swing the camera up defensively just as he heard something in the grotto's water. He couldn't see anything except the white spots before his eyes.

"Well, now!" The stranger seemed amused. "The kid's got spunk! Not much sense, but plenty of spunk!"

"I warned you!" Josh cried, facing the man and swinging the camera by the straps. Josh could barely make out the man's form through the dancing white spots in front of his eyes.

He did better seeing in the sunlight from the hole in the ceiling. Josh saw his father's long red rope hanging there. An idea snapped into place.

Josh thought, "If I can just get the stranger close enough to this rope, I can grab it, give it a yank and maybe knock him off his feet." Aloud, he said, "I can't see!"

The stranger gave a short cry of triumph and started forward, his right hand outstretched to grab the camera. "I told you! One kid can't do anything!"

Josh watched the stranger nearing the rope. In another second, he'd be close enough for Josh to try.

The stranger commanded, "Now, give me that..."

He broke off and whirled to face the grotto.

Josh did the same. He had heard something a moment ago! Now he could see well enough to know two people were crawling out of the water onto the cave floor.

"Tank! Roger!"

"Sure t'ing, Bruddah!" Roger answered.

"It's us," Tank said.

The stranger flipped his light at both boys, but they

were ready. They had seen what had happened to Josh. They shielded their eyes with their hands.

The stranger almost laughed. "Well, now! More kids! I can still handle all three of you!"

Josh set the camera on the cave floor and bent over his father to free his hands, just as Mr. Ladd strained mightily against his loosened bonds.

"There!" The rope fell free. Mr. Ladd leaped up and faced the stranger. "Mister, now you've got three kids and one very angry father!"

The stranger whirled and ran toward the rope dangling in the shaft of sunlight from the opening in the roof.

Josh was faster. "Oh, no you don't!" He stooped down and grabbed the trailing end of the rope. He yanked yard, catching the man behind the knees. He fell backward onto the cave floor.

"Quick!" Josh yelled, giving the rope a quick throw around the man's wet-suited legs. "Grab him!"

"With pleasure, Son!" Mr. Ladd replied. He caught the stranger's flailing right wrist and brought it up behind his back in an arm lock.

At the same instant, all three boys converged on the stranger. In moments, he was securely tied.

They all stood, shouting happy congratulations at each other.

Mr. Ladd was standing fully in the beam of sunlight from the ceiling when his eyes met Josh's. For a moment, the boy saw the happy look in his father's face. Then, slowly, his eyes firmed and his mouth closed in a hard line.

Josh thought, "Oh, no! Now I'm really going to get it!"

Chapter Twelve

BEYOND THE SECRET

"**J**oshua Andrew Ladd," Mr. Ladd spoke quietly so the others couldn't hear. "You did some quick thinking a few minutes ago. Maybe you even saved my life. I'm grateful to you and your friends."

Josh swallowed hard, barely nodding, knowing that when either of his parents used his full name, he was in big trouble. He waited in dread of what was coming.

"But," Mr. Ladd continued, "you disobeyed me! You risked your life and the lives of those boys! I told you to stay with the girls! Where are they?"

Josh could see his father was very angry and upset, barely keeping his voice under control. The boy had to swallow twice before he could explain about Tiffany's Portuguese man-of-war sting and treatment. He added, "But they'll be okay! Probably back on the beach waiting for us right now!"

Mr. Ladd nodded. "I pray they are! We'd better go check right now." He lowered his voice even more so Tank and Roger couldn't possibly hear. "But we're not through with this conversation, young man! We'll finish it later, in private!"

Some time later, Mr. Ladd and the three boys had raised the stranger through the cave roof with the long rope. Now that he was a prisoner, he seemed resigned and didn't resist.

Mr. Ladd asked, "Who are you? And how'd you know I had a map to this place?"

"William Arthur Crandall," the stranger replied. "Former employee of the *National Historical Journal* in Los Angeles."

Mr. Ladd snapped his fingers. "So that's it!"

Crandall nodded. "I saw you the day the editor gave you the article assignment on this place.

"Unfortunately, just before you arrived, he fired me. I'd been stealing photos and things from the files, and selling the stuff to a competitor magazine.

"I had already lifted the photographs of you and the Shark Pit but didn't get a chance to photocopy the map before I was forced to leave the building."

He shrugged resignedly and looked down at his bound hands. "If you and these kids hadn't messed things up, I'd have been rich from selling all that stuff from the cave."

Mr. Ladd said grimly, "Well, you're going to jail for burglarizing our hotel room and stealing the map! I hope they extradite you to California on charges of burglarizing my home and classroom, too!"

Mr. Ladd turned to the three boys. "Okay, let's go check on the girls."

As they started away from the cave, Josh glanced back. He realized why nobody had found the entrance since the old Hawaiian had accidentally stumbled into it more than sixty years before. The entrance was totally hidden in dense brush. Without the map, it might never have been found.

The stranger protested, "You're not going to go away and leave all that stuff? It must be priceless!"

Mr. Ladd said, "It'll be safe! We'll come back and recover it all later. It's been there about two hundred years, I'd guess. But that cave is on state land, not private property. So anything found there belongs to Hawaii, not to the finder. Besides, it's part of the Hawaiians' heritage from their ancestors."

With the aid of the map Mr. Ladd had recovered from Crandall, the party moved fairly rapidly back toward the black sand beach.

Mr. Ladd walked through the dense undergrowth, followed single-file by the prisoner, Josh, Tank and Roger.

Crandall turned in the narrow trail to look at Josh. "Kid, before I jumped your father when he came sliding down that rope into the cave, I'd already seen things that convinced me this was a historic discovery. Like that full-length, red-and-yellow feather cape. It must be worth a fortune!"

Josh's father raised his voice while keeping his eyes on the trail. "That's a feathered mantle. It took thousands of birds to make the cape, because each bird only had a couple of either the red or the yellow feathers. I believe the birds are now extinct."

Roger called from the rear of the column, "That cape in the cave looks just like the one used on all the visitor signs in Hawaii."

Josh asked, "Isn't that supposed to be like the one King Kamehameha* wore?"

The stranger spoke enthusiastically. "That's the one! Those were only worn by ancient Hawaiian alii*. Maybe this one belonged to ol' King Kam himself."

Mr. Ladd twisted his head to say, "I'm sure you know he means the chieftain who unified all the islands back in the early 1800s."

Tank asked Crandall, "What makes you think that one was his?"

Crandall snorted. "That cave was filled with artifacts that could have only belonged to the highest alii. That's why all those kapu sticks were everywhere. And nobody was higher in rank than Kamehameha himself."

Mr. Ladd was thoughtful. "Well, we'll find out when the experts at the Bishop Museum check it out."

The stranger continued, "And those bones! Did you see them, kid?"

Josh nodded, still feeling a little squeamish about the skeleton.

The stranger added, "Those are not only human bones, but they might even be the great King Kam's himself!"

Mr. Ladd mused, "I thought I read where the experts think his bones were hidden on the Big Island of Hawaii."

The stranger shrugged. "Who knows? His burial place was secret back when he died, so maybe his bones were hidden on Maui—maybe right in that very cave!"

The map Mr. Ladd recovered from the stranger helped the party find their way quickly to the black sand beach. As they started through the palms at the edge of the little beach, Josh heard his sister's voice.

"There they are!" he cried, breaking into a run toward Tiffany. Marsha was with her. Josh had never been so glad to see his sister in his life, but she wasn't happy with him.

"Where have you been?" Tiffany demanded, turning to face him. Her skin was still red from the sting, but she didn't seem to be in pain anymore. "We've been worried sick!"

"Yes," Marsha added, glaring at Tank. "We thought you had all drow...drow..." Her voice broke and she couldn't say the word.

Josh asked, "Didn't you find our note?"

"What note?" Tiffany asked, then seemed to see the stranger for the first time. "Who's he?" she asked.

Mr. Ladd explained briefly about the cave and what had happened, with Tank and Roger joining in. Josh didn't feel like talking. His mind was still on what his father would do when discipline time came.

"All right," Mr. Ladd said at last, "That's enough explanation for now. Get your things and let's start back to the car. Then we'll stop at that little store and call the authorities so they can take Mr. Crandall off our hands."

In the walk from the black sand beach toward the station wagon, Mr. Ladd explained why he had taken the overland route to the cave.

"When I saw those Hawaiian words on the map, I knew I didn't want to go by the cove."

Tank said, "We read those words but don't know what they mean! Mano something."

Mr. Ladd explained, "Mano means shark in Hawaiian, and ki'owai means pool. Shark Pool or Shark Pit."

Tank groaned. "Shark Pit! I wish we'd known that before we got into that place!"

As they got back into the station wagon Mr. Ladd had rented, Josh asked Crandall, "How'd you ever find us after we lost you in traffic that day at the airport?"

"Easy! I had spotted your bags on the carousel at the airport before you saw them. I took a look at the tags and got the name of the hotel where you were going to stay. Later, I watched it, broke in, got the map and found the burial chamber with its historic treasure."

Tank said, "I'd rather have found pirates' gold, or a chest of jewels, or at least some black pearls."

After the deputies took the stranger away, Mr. Ladd

drove the station wagon back to Lahaina. He paid for the lost snorkel mouthpiece and the fin the shark had taken, telling Josh those items would come out of his allowance.

Then they picked up Mrs. Ladd, Mrs. Catlett and Josh's little brother, and returned to Honolulu.

The next evening the family sat on the lanai outside the parents' hotel room. They were resting from packing for the trip to California.

Mrs. Ladd said, "In a way, I dread having to return to the Mainland to pack our belongings, put our house up for sale, and do all those other details. But this place is so beautiful it's worth the trouble."

Tiffany swung her arms wide. "Oh, it's going to be incredible! I'll be with Marsha every day! And Josh will be with Tank and probably Roger."

Mr. Ladd said, "Thanks to the money from the magazine article, we'll have enough to help buy a weekly newspaper so we can make a living here."

"Speaking of newspapers," Mrs. Ladd said, reaching over to a side table, "here's a stack of local papers Barbara Catlett and the Okamotos saved for us about your experience in the Shark Pit. Our friends and neighbors back home will want to read what happened to all of you."

Josh stirred uncomfortably as his mother held up a front page and read parts of the story aloud. "What is being called a 'major historic discovery' was made this week when some adventuresome boys and two men found a Maui grotto and burial chamber filled with artifacts and bones which are being examined to see if they are those of the great King Kamehameha."

Mrs. Ladd read on. The article said the State of Hawaii was grateful for the discovery of the priceless relics which ancient Hawaiians had hidden in the cave about two centuries ago. According to the paper, the experts had not reached a conclusion, but if it was decided the feathered mantle really had belonged to King Kamehameha, there would be a substantial reward for Mr. Ladd and the boys.

The uncertainty of his discipline kept Josh subdued until the morning the Ladds were to fly back to the Mainland. Josh and his little brother had just finished closing their last suitcase when Mr. Ladd entered the room. One look at his face told Josh that the time had come.

Mr. Ladd sent Nathan next door to watch for the Catletts to arrive and take them to the airport. When the little boy had closed the door behind him, Mr. Ladd sat down on the edge of the bed. Josh saw that his father held the lightweight brown Bible he carried when he traveled.

His father indicated that Josh should sit on the upholstered chair beside the bed. The boy gulped and sat down slowly, his eyes downcast.

Mr. Ladd spoke softly, almost sadly. "Son, you hurt your mother and me very deeply when you disobeyed us. In addition to almost losing your own life, you risked the lives of others. Just because it turned out fairly well doesn't excuse what you did, or free you from discipline. We love you, but we don't like what you did. Do you understand?"

Josh didn't raise his head, but nodded and spoke in a very low voice. "Yes, Dad."

Out of the corner of his eye Josh saw the Bible, as his dad continued. "This Book," he said, "lists 'Honor your father and your mother' as one of the Ten Commandments. Do you recall that?"

"Yes."

"It also says, 'Children, obey your parents in the Lord.' Remember?"

Josh nodded.

Mr. Ladd reached out and gently lifted his son's chin so their eyes met.

"Your mother and I believe that God gave you to us as a sacred trust. We've tried to teach you what's right, but if you choose to disobey, we all lose. You nearly died out there along with Tank and Roger, because they followed your lead—and your example was wrong!"

"I...I know. I'm sorry. I'll never do it again, Dad."

Josh felt his father's hand tremble slightly against his chin. "Thank you, Son." The words were barely audible. "I believe you, and we'll say nothing more about this incident after your first month in Hawaii is spent without one privilege with Tank or Roger. You're restricted to family activities, or things we do with the Catletts or Okamotos as families."

"Aw, Dad! A whole month..."

"Is that understood?" Mr. Ladd said, his eyes firmly locked on the boy's.

Slowly, Josh nodded. "Yes." Inside himself, he knew he deserved every bit of that discipline.

"Good!" Mr. Ladd stood up, tucked the Bible under his arm and put his forearms around his son. Gently, he lifted Josh to his feet and hugged him hard.

The Okamotos followed the Catletts in their station wagon to the airport. There, the departing Ladd family was again laden with colorful and fragrant leis.

While they waited for their flight to be announced, Mrs. Catlett said, "There's one part about this whole mystery I still don't understand—about the old Hawaiian man who gave the map to Tank and Roger."

Mr. Ladd finished rechecking his ticket envelope before answering. "The old Hawaiian had long before showed the map to his grandson—his only living relative—but he didn't act on it because of the kapu, the taboo. They were really afraid.

"But after his grandfather gave it to Tank and Roger, the grandson got concerned. He'd had photocopies made some time before, and sent one of those to the historical magazine because his teacher was a subscriber. And that's where I came in."

Tiffany adjusted her flight bag on her shoulder. "Well, it all turned out okay! The Hawaiians get back their relics. Dad and the boys got their names in the paper. The stranger went to jail for burglarizing our hotel room. Dad gets the money for the magazine article. And so we can all move here to live."

Roger's normal shyness around Tiffany and Marsha made him lean over and whisper to Josh and Tank, "We going to have planty fun! Shark Pit was nothing! I know planty moh we can do together, Bruddahs! You ever been to a volcano when it's erupting?"

Josh said, "I won't be allowed to do anything for a month after we move here. But it'll make it easier to think about the fun we can have together after that."

Mr. Ladd shot a hard look at his son, who added quickly, "But I'm never again going to make the mistake I did this time!"

His father's look softened and he smiled slightly. Josh's eyes quickly moved around the circle of family and friends. They smiled back.

Their flight was called and Josh stood for a final round of goodbyes. But the Ladd family would soon be back, and Josh knew more exciting adventures would be waiting, beginning with a volcano.

THE LEGEND OF FIRE
by Lee Roddy

There's more trouble in paradise! Introducing Book Two in the *Ladd Family Adventure* Series from Focus on the Family Publishing.

What begins as a relaxing day on Hawaii's Kona Coast quickly becomes a roller coaster adventure as Josh unsuspectingly plunges the Ladd Family into the greatest danger of their lives.

Through all of the up-and-down, heart-pounding struggles, including the valiant attempt to rescue his kidnapped father from the path of an erupting volcano, Josh learns the true meaning of family and the importance of sticking together in times of crisis.

Available at your local Christian bookstore, or write to Focus on the Family, Pomona, CA 91799.

PUBLISHING   ISBN 0-8499-3896-1

Chapter One

Haole: *(how-lee)* A Hawaiian word originally mean ing "stranger" but now used to mean Caucasians, or white people.

Kamaaina: *(kham-ah-eye-nah)* A Hawaiian word meaning "child of the land," or native.

Sibling: *(sib-ling)* A brother or sister.

Chapter Two

Aloha: *(ah-low-hah)* A very practical Hawaiian word with varied meanings, including hello, goodbye and love.

Aloha shirt: A loose-fitting man's Hawaiian shirt worn outside the pants. The garment is usually very colorful.

Free-lance: *(free-lance)* Someone not on a regular salary, such as a writer who works for more than one employer.

Frequent flyer: *(freee-kwunt flyer)* An airline bonus

program whereby extra benefits are offered to persons who fly a lot. This may include free trips after a passenger has flown a certain number of miles.

Hibiscus: *(hi-bis-cus)* Hawaii's state flower. It has a large, open blossom and is available in many colors. No particular color is designated for the state flower, however.

Koolau Range: *(koh-oh-lau [as in ow!]* range*)* The volcanic mountains rising directly behind Honolulu.

Lava tubes: *(lah-vuh* tubes*)* The outside lava hardens first, forming a crust through which the hot, interior lava flows. Eventually, most of the lava drains out of the inside, leaving a tunnel or tube. These may be up to fifty feet in diameter.

Leis: *(laze)* Necklaces of flowers which are given to people on arrival to Hawaii and sometimes on departure.

Mug book: Police and other authorities maintain bust, or "mug," photographs of arrested persons so that victims may look through the books in an effort to recognize someone who may have committed a crime against them.

Muumuu: *(moo-oo-moo-oo)* This word is sometimes mispronounced as moo-moo. It is a colorful loose dress or gown which is frequently worn by women in Hawaii.

Plumeria: *(ploo-mar-y-ah)* Also called frangipani (*fran-jee-pan-ee*) A shrub or small tree which produces large, very fragrant blossoms. They are popular in leis.

Tetanus: (*tet-ah-nus*) An infectious disease sometimes called lockjaw. It is caused by a bacterium entering the body through wounds.

Ukulele: (*commonly yoo-keh-lay-lee, but in Hawaii: ooh-coo-lay-lay*) It literally means "flea," but is commonly used today to refer to a small, guitar-like instrument with four strings.

Chapter Three

Pidgin English: (*pidj-uhn* english) A simplified version of English. It was originally used in parts of the Orient for communication between people who spoke with different languages.

Windward: (*wind-word*) The direction from which the wind blows. The opposite of leeward.

Chapter Four

Bananas: (*buh-nan-uhs*) Bananas in Hawaii grow in small shrubs or trees with long, wide leaves. These bananas are used mostly for cooking.

Bougainvillea: (*boo-gun-vil-ee-yah*) An ornamental vine with small, colored flowers.

Buddhist: (*bood-uhst*) A person who follows the religion growing out of the teaching of Gautama Buddha.

Caucasian: (*kaw-kay-zjun*) People of the white race.

Doxology: *(dahk-sahl-uh-jee)* A hymn beginning, "Praise God from Whom all blessings flow. . . ."

Kapu: *(kah-poo)* A warning which means taboo, forbidden or keep out in Hawaiian.

Snorkeling: *(snor-kel-ing)* The name given to a system swimmers use to breathe through a small tube while their faces are under the surface. A face mask allows excellent visibility for "eyeballing" or seeing small fish almost eye-to-eye.

Ti: *(tee)* This plant has long, slender, green leaves. They are used as skirts by the hula dancers who entertain visitors. Although many mainlanders and songs refer to the dancers wearing "grass skirts," they are really ti leaves.

Chapter Five

Conch Shell: *(kahnch* shell*)* A spiral seashell which is large enough to be used as a horn or trumpet.

Haleakala Crater: *(hah-lay-ah-kah-la* crater*)* This literally means, "House of the sun." A national park, this 3,000-foot-deep crater on the island of Maui is located in a dormant volcano. The crater covers 19 square miles. It is 21 miles around, 2½ miles wide and 7½ miles long.

Lanai: *(luh-niy)* Porch.

Malihini: *(mah-lah-hee-nee)* Newcomer.

Roadstead anchorage: *(rode-sted* anchorage*)* A nautical term used to describe where ships anchor.

Less enclosed than a harbor.

Tiki torch: *(tee-kee* torch*)* An ornamental torch which uses an oil-based fuel with a live flame that will not blow out in the winds.

Chapter Six

Akamai: *(Ah-kah-my)* Smart, intelligent.

Heiau: *(hay-ow)* Ancient pagan temple grounds where the Hawaiians held religious services.

Huhu: *(hoo-hoo)* Angry.

Kahuna: *(kah-hoo-nah)* A Hawaiian priest representing the ancient or traditional beliefs.

Kiawe: *(kay-ah-vay)* A very thorny tree that grows as tall as a house.

Chapter Seven

Da kine: *(dah kine)* Pidgin for "the kind." This is more of an expression and is therefore not usually translated literally.

Pupule: *(poo-poo-lay)* Crazy.

Chapter Eight

Mano: *(mahn-oh)* Shark.

Ki'owai: *(kee-oh-why-ee)* Pool.

Hale pule: *(hah-lay poo-lay)* This literally means "church house." In general usage it generally refers to a church.

Chapter Nine

Cinder Cone: *(sin-der* cone*)* Coarse residue expelled from a volcano that forms a broad-based cone which narrows toward the top.

Chapter Twelve

King Kamehameha: *(*king *kuh-may-hah-may-hah)* The chief who unified all of the Hawaiian islands and became their first king.

Alii: *(Ah-lee-ee)* Hawaiian royalty.